APPLYING AN INDUSTRY
BEST PRACTICE TO DoD
BUSINESS PROCESS
REENGINEERING

ACTIVITY BASED COSTING

& Performance
A B C & P

KAREN B. BURK
DOUGLAS W. WEBSTER, Ph.D.

© American Management Systems, Inc. 1994
Fairfax, Virginia

Suggested cataloging information:

Webster, Douglas W.
  Activity Based Costing and Performance

  Includes bibliographies and indexes
  ISBN 0-922255-01-6
  1. Cost Management 2. Activity-Based Costing 3. Activity-Based Management 4. Cost Accounting
  I. Burk, Karen B.
HF5686.C8W392
657.42—dc20

Cover and Graphic Design: W.E.Tiller.

A C K N O W L E D G E M E N T S

A   B   C   &   P

This book represents a common vision of several people who contributed to its completion. That vision was to present the benefits of Activity-Based Costing and Performance, so beneficially applied in the commercial sector, to motivate managers in the Department of Defense.

Mr. Mike Yoemans and Mr. Dave Norem of the Office of the Secretary of Defense, helped identify DoD's specific needs for information on Activity-Based Costing as related to Business Process Reengineering. We also appreciate the reviews and comments of Mr. Paul Strassmann, former Director of Defense Information, Office of the Secretary of Defense, Dr. C. J. McNair, professor of accounting at Babson College, Mr. Frank Bankes, manager of the program to reengineer the naval shipyards, and several others within the Department of Defense whose guidance and suggestions helped shape the final product. We also appreciate those who took the time to share with us their experiences in implementing ABC within the Defense environment: Mr. Russ Melroy at the Defense General Supply Center, Mr. Leo Oswalt at the U. S. Army Center for Public Works, and Mr. Oswalt's support contractor at Management Analysis, Inc.

We would like to thank several of our colleagues at American Management Systems, Inc. for their significant contributions to the content and style of this book. Ms. Christine Walsh conducted extensive research and drafted much of the material relating to the fundamentals of ABC&P and to how the results can be used to design new business practices. Ms. Sarah Hill also provided research assistance and helped create the case study example woven throughout the book. Ms. Sarah Casseday provided expertise in cost-benefit analyses, reviewed several drafts, and was instrumental in getting this book to press. Mr. W. Eugene Tiller, our graphics designer, took our scribbles and sketches and created a professional and attractive work. Ms. Lisa Turner and Ms. Bernice Parent provided substantial editing support, turning our thoughts into clear and concise prose. Mr. Leif Ulstrup and Mr. Scott Price reviewed drafts and helped us form and shape our ideas. And, finally, Mr. Kevin Moriarty and Mr. Michael Long shared their experiences with DoD functional managers and helped transform our ideas into practical guidance.

TABLE OF CONTENTS

INTRODUCTION

1	**INTRODUCTION**
2	ABC&P and BPR
4	Linking ABC&P to the Steps of BPR
5	ABC&P and Government Accounting
5	ABC&P in the Context of Ongoing Operations
6	A Reader's Guide: Organization of this Book

CHAPTER 1

11	**THE FUNDAMENTALS OF ABC&P**
11	ABC&P as a Tool for BPR
12	– Insights Into the Costs Incurred by Activities and Products
12	– Insights Into the Factors that Drive Costs
12	– Insights Into Performance
13	The Components of ABC&P
13	– Cost Component
16	– Performance Component
18	ABC&P and Traditional Costing Approaches
18	Summary

CHAPTER 2

23	**ESTABLISHING THE PROJECT FRAMEWORK**
23	Assess the Appropriateness of ABC&P for the Project
24	Gain Support from Stakeholders
25	Evaluate the Availability of Data and Sources
26	– Documentation
26	– Interviews
27	– Questionnaires
27	– Workshops
28	– Other Alternatives
28	Define the Project Approach
28	– Purpose
28	– Objectives
29	– Scope
29	– Major Phases/Tasks
31	– Schedule Constraints
31	Determine the Level of Effort Required
31	Form and Train the ABC&P Team
34	Summary

TABLE OF CONTENTS

CHAPTER 3

37 ESTABLISHING THE ABC&P BASELINE

37 Understand Activity Model Basics

38 – A Useful Activity Model

38 – The Need for an Activity Model

39 – Designing an Activity Model

40 Develop the As-Is Activity Model

42 Identify All ABC&P Components

44 – Product(s)

45 – Activities

47 – Resources

47 – Resource and Activity Drivers

50 – Cost Drivers

52 – Performance Measures

54 Collect Data

54 – Time Period for Data Collection

55 – Available Sources

56 – Cost Type

57 – Level of Cost Aggregation

58 Calculate Activity Costs

61 Calculate Product Costs

63 – Distinguish Among Primary, Secondary, and Sustaining Activities

64 – Assign Secondary Activity Costs to Primary Activities

65 – Assign Primary Activity Costs to Products

69 Summary

CHAPTER 4

73 USING ABC&P RESULTS TO DESIGN NEW BUSINESS PRACTICES

73 Focus the Improvement Effort on High Impact Activities

74 – Pareto Analysis

74 – Interrelationship Diagrams

77 Analyze Improvement Opportunities

77 – Paradigm Analysis

79 – Value-Added Analysis

84 – Benchmarking

87 – Best Practices Analysis

88 Develop and Analyze To-Be Models

89 – Developing To-Be Models

90 – Dynamic Simulation in Model Analysis

93 Summary

T A B L E   O F   C O N T E N T S

C H A P T E R   5

97	**USING ABC&P TO SELECT ALTERNATIVES**
97	Prepare for Your CBA
98	– CBA Objectives
98	– The Role of ABC&P in CBA
99	– Level of Analysis Required
101	Estimate Costs and Benefits for Each Alternative
102	– Assess the Impacts of Process Changes
104	– Estimate To-Be Activity Costs
108	Compare Costs and Benefits of Alternatives to the As-Is
108	Select the Best Alternative
109	Summary

C H A P T E R   6

113	**MAKING IMPROVEMENTS SUCCEED**
113	Formalize New Processes
114	– Define Detailed Specifications and Procedures for New Processes
114	– Motivate and Train Personnel
115	– Establish a New Organizational Structure
116	Fine Tune Reengineered Processes
116	Lock In BPR Gains
116	– Align Culture with New Business Practices
117	– Establish a System for Measuring BPR Results
118	– Align Performance Measures with New Business Practices
119	– Initiate Program for Continuous Improvement
119	Reimplement BPR as Necessary
120	Summary

E P I L O G U E

123	**WHAT THE FUTURE HOLDS**
123	Step Beyond Cost Analysis
124	Improve Cost Collection and Reporting
126	Encourage Strategic Management
127	Align Budgets
127	Maximize Process Management
128	Summary

R E F E R E N C E S

F U R T H E R   R E A D I N G S

G L O S S A R Y

I N D E X

Introduction

INTRODUCTION

Both public and private sector organizations are using business process reengineering (BPR) to achieve significant improvements in the way they conduct business. Successful BPR efforts usually have two goals: cost improvement and performance improvement.

Activity-Based Costing & Performance (ABC&P) enables managers to better understand the dynamics of cost and performance and the role they play in BPR. ABC&P extends the power of activity-based costing by adding the dimension of activity performance. This dimension focuses on non-financial aspects of business operations such as customer satisfaction and rework. In the context of BPR, ABC&P provides the framework for recognizing high impact areas for improvement and for monitoring improvement gains over time.

ABC&P helps you better understand the dynamics of cost and performance and the role they play in BPR.

ABC&P adapts the best business practice of activity-based costing specifically for Department of Defense (DoD) managers involved in BPR efforts. In the DoD environment, the pressure on you to control costs while continuing to meet performance goals is exacerbated by budget reductions, hiring freezes, and regulatory pressures. At the same time, you are dealing with the pains of downsizing, and sometimes also having to compete with your counterparts in other agencies and in the private sector as fee-for-service and outsourcing strategies take hold.

ABC&P AND BPR

BPR can help you compete with the private sector and improve the efficiency and effectiveness of your enterprise's business practices. BPR involves carefully examining the way you currently perform business processes, evaluating alternatives for improving or streamlining current processes, and selecting and implementing new processes. BPR also involves examining the impact of technology, organizational structure, and culture on your business practices. In the course of the effort you will model your current processes and alternative future processes in a way that is designed to facilitate improvements. You may also investigate other business enterprises performing similar processes to learn what works well for them and how different ways of doing business affect competitiveness or efficiency. BPR efforts typically involve adopting principles that are at the core of successful business strategies: a customer focus, built-in quality, and efficient use of resources.

Over the years DoD has faced many budget cutting or downsizing initiatives and met these challenges by "tightening its belt" rather than making genuine improvements. Generally, the way to meet reductions was left to the imagination of individual managers. One department or agency might initiate reductions-in-force, another might freeze capital investments. Current downsizing initiatives are not only a reaction to government spending cuts, but also a reflection of the changing role of national defense in response to the new world order. DoD is reexamining its mission and the functions it performs in support of that mission. DoD is also taking the time to examine the way private companies have streamlined their business processes, and has adopted best business practices in developing a process improvement methodology for DoD functional managers. That methodology includes examining and evaluating current practices and analyzing the possibilities for change.

Where does ABC&P fit in? ABC&P provides insights into the costs that go into the products of a business process and the drivers that affect its performance. When used with BPR, ABC&P enables the manager to quickly identify areas for improvement and to reengineer where there is a high pay-back potential. Specifically ABC&P does the following:

- Identifies the resources consumed in performing activities and the factors driving resource consumption
- Defines the relationship between business activities and the cost of products and services
- Measures the performance of activities and identifies the factors driving performance

By itself, BPR allows managers to examine business processes from an efficiency standpoint, primarily performance-based analysis. By modeling processes, you can target inefficiencies, duplicative processes, and opportunities for streamlining. Some opportunities are not as evident as others, however, and modeling and analyzing processes is a time-intensive endeavor. By incorporating ABC&P into BPR, you will be able to more quickly identify resource-consuming activities within your business processes that can be reengineered to produce real savings. This will increase the probability of achieving significant gains from your BPR effort.

After identifying the area you want to reengineer, ABC&P will help you estimate, understand, and measure the tangible impacts of reengineering. ABC&P adds depth and understanding to many BPR techniques such as value-added analysis, benchmarking, and cost-benefit analysis. It does this by demonstrating the drivers and rationale for resource consumption and providing a way to monitor cost and performance. At the start of your BPR effort, make a list of the approaches you will be taking and the techniques you will use to examine your current business processes and develop new ones. Wherever BPR techniques focus on cost or performance improvements, it is likely that ABC&P can play a role.

For example, if you decide to benchmark your process against how well it is performed in other organizations, ABC&P will provide a basis for comparison. Benchmarking is basically a comparison of performance designed to highlight opportunities for improvement. Recognizing and knowing the reasons for activity cost and performance drivers will help you differentiate between the way your process is performed and the way a

ABC&P helps in estimating, understanding, and measuring the tangible impacts of reengineering when used in conjunction with BPR techniques such as value-added analysis, benchmarking, and cost-benefit analysis.

similar process is performed in another organization. You will better understand which process changes will have a significant impact, how efficiencies are achieved in other organizations, and whether such practices can be adopted by your organization.

After you implement changes, you can use ABC&P to measure progress. In almost all BPR efforts, some gains are not as great as expected and others turn out to be better. With ABC&P, you can monitor the costs of your reengineered effort in a manner that allows a direct correlation between the old and new processes, and between expected results and actual results.

LINKING ABC&P TO THE STEPS OF BPR

ABC&P provides a direct correlation between the old process and the new, and between expected results and actual results.

BPR has many synonyms: business process redesign, functional process improvement, and other generic terms as well as several proprietary names meaning the same thing. Whatever it is called, BPR involves analyzing current business practices, the "As-Is" environment, and evaluating alternatives to making those practices more effective and more efficient in the "To-Be" environment.

In the same way that BPR is often called by many names, it also has specific steps that are often defined in different ways. This book parallels the following steps in DoD's guidance for process improvement:[1]

- Establish Functional Project Framework
- Document and Analyze Current Baseline
- Perform Business Improvement Analysis
- Develop Management Plan and Functional Economic Analysis
- Review and Approve Program
- Execute Functional Process Improvement Program Decisions

ABC&P plays a role in each of these steps. As described in the next section, this book is designed to "walk through" a typical BPR implementation project in a manner that correlates with the BPR steps. A high-level model of ABC&P as related to the DoD BPR steps is shown in **Exhibit I-1**.

---

[1] *Corporate Information Management: Process Improvement Methodology for DoD Functional Managers.*, D. Appleton Company, Inc. (Fairfax, 1993.) pg. 9-10.

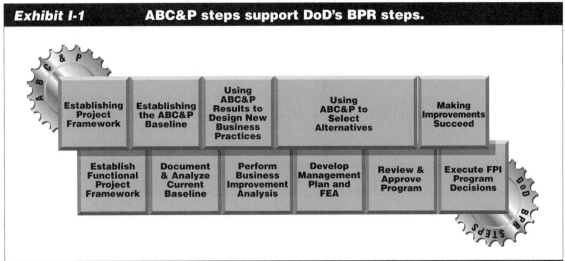

Exhibit I-1   ABC&P steps support DoD's BPR steps.

ABC&P AND GOVERNMENT ACCOUNTING

While many businesses have adopted activity-based costing to replace their traditional accounting methods, the government has not. ABC&P provides a framework for you as a DoD manager to work within the government accounting system in a way that complements its purpose. Simply put, ABC&P adds a new perspective. It allows costs to be allocated in a way that is meaningful in terms of the functions you must oversee. Because ABC&P incorporates performance as well as costs, it becomes a tool by which both functional and financial managers can evaluate the effectiveness of their investments.

Exhibit I-2 illustrates the complementary role that ABC&P provides in the government accounting environment.

ABC&P IN THE CONTEXT OF ONGOING OPERATIONS

This book is primarily directed at ABC&P's role in BPR. ABC&P can also play a role in other areas of management practice:

- In *performance measurement*, ABC&P enables cost and non-financial measurements for activities and for products and services.
- For *strategic planning*, ABC&P provides visibility into the link between strategic goals and investments.
- Used in *investment strategy*, ABC&P gives insights into the relationship among resources, activities, and products or services that can lead to identifying new opportunities.

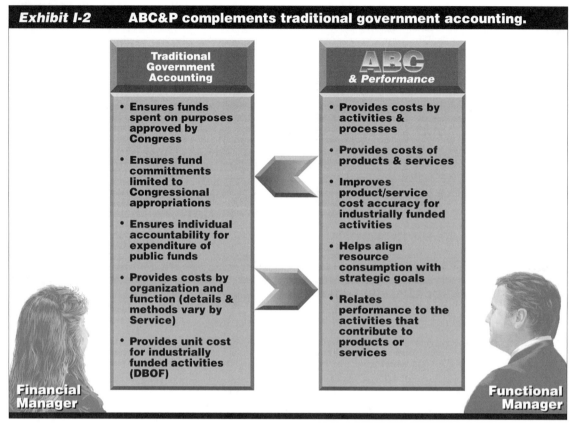

Exhibit I-2   **ABC&P complements traditional government accounting.**

- In *accounting and budgeting*, ABC&P improves the accuracy of reporting the costs of products and services and helps in estimating future requirements.
- For *product and service evaluations*, ABC&P enhances analysis of production costs and can facilitate pricing of products and services.

Maximizing the gains of BPR involves a continuous process made up of the areas above. These are the management practices that keep well designed business processes performing at their peak by responding to change, customer demand, and emerging priorities. The principles of ABC&P that apply during the reengineering effort also apply for ongoing process management.

A READER'S GUIDE: ORGANIZATION OF THIS BOOK

This book gives an overview of ABC&P and explains its use in BPR projects and continuous improvement. The wheel shown in **Exhibit I-3** provides the framework for the organization of this book. The chapters of the book are represented by the spokes which link ABC&P to the BPR steps.

Chapter 1, "The Fundamentals of ABC&P," provides an overview of the basic concepts of ABC&P. For those familiar with activity-based costing, this chapter may cover familiar ground. However, ABC&P adds the element of activity-based performance, which is described in the chapter.

Chapters 2 through 6 correlate to the steps in ABC&P:

- Establishing the Project Framework
- Establishing the ABC&P Baseline
- Using ABC&P Results to Design New Business Practices

Exhibit I-3   **ABC&P is the hub for BPR.**

- Using ABC&P to Select Alternatives
- Making Improvements Succeed

These chapters provide "how to" information to enable you to get the most from ABC&P within the context of BPR. An abbreviated case study has been included in these chapters to highlight specific steps of ABC&P and provide its relationship to a fictitious BPR project.

Although this book concentrates on ABC&P as used during BPR efforts, BPR itself looks beyond quick fixes to continuous process improvement. Likewise, ABC&P has an important role as an ongoing management tool that enables managers to maintain strategic direction in evaluating their business performance. The Epilogue, "What the Future Holds," examines ABC&P in this role.

The appendices included in this book are intended to provide supplementary information and reference material. This book assumes a fundamental knowledge of BPR and management practices. However, references are provided for additional reading on those topics as well as to identify sources of information on activity-based costing. A glossary of significant terms is also included.

The definition and use of terms in this book are consistent with those found in the Computer-Aided Manufacturing-International (CAM-I)[2] Glossary of Activity-Based Management (ABM). CAM-I is the non-profit research organization that initiated the Cost Management System (CMS) program to promote collaborative research in management accounting.

---

[2] *The CAM-I Glossary of Activity-Based Management*, Edited by Norm Raffish and Peter B.B. Turney, (Arlington: CAM-I, 1991.)

CHAPTER

1

ABC
Performance

The
Fundamentals
of ABC&P

Method goes far to prevent trouble in business; for it makes the task easy, hinders confusion, saves abundance of time and instructs those who have business.

– WILLIAM PENN

CHAPTER 1: THE FUNDAMENTALS OF ABC&P

ABC&P is a methodology you can use to identify and measure the costs and evaluate the performance of your organization's business processes. This chapter addresses the following fundamentals of this book:

- How to use ABC&P as a tool for BPR
- The basic components of ABC&P and the relationship among the components
- The difference between ABC&P and traditional costing approaches

ABC&P AS A TOOL FOR BPR

BPR is an approach for improving the way your business performs processes to better meet your strategic objectives. ABC&P is a tool for BPR that provides you with a means of pinpointing the areas and causes of poor performance, and targeting efforts on these improvement opportunities. Specifically, ABC&P provides insights into the following areas: the costs incurred by activities and products, the factors that drive those costs, and activity performance. Understanding the costs of activities and products

ABC&P provides insights into activity costs, product costs, factors that drive costs, and performance.

will help you focus your BPR effort on high pay-back areas and target investments to support continuous improvement. By using ABC&P to evaluate the performance of activities that compose processes, you can better understand the reasons your organization consumes resources, and the effects of one activity's performance on other activities within your organization's processes.

Insights Into the Costs Incurred by Activities and Products

ABC&P provides accurate cost calculations for activities and products. ABC&P calculations in turn provide information on whether or not your resource consumption is consistent with your organization's objectives. These objectives may include customer satisfaction, product quality, and level of readiness. Opportunities for improvement exist where inconsistencies between resource consumption and business objectives occur.

Insights Into the Factors that Drive Costs

ABC&P provides insights into the factors that drive costs. Before you can change the way you perform a business process you must understand *how* and *why* your organization uses resources. Reducing resources without first changing the behaviors that cause the consumption of these resources is analogous to treating the symptoms of an illness rather than treating the illness itself. To achieve lasting results from improvement efforts, you must change the factors that cause costs to be incurred. Understanding the factors that drive your costs allows you to deal with the causes and effects of your resource consumption. Insights alone do not achieve cost savings. Resources must be redeployed or eliminated to translate these insights into actual savings.

Insights Into Performance

ABC&P provides both financial and non-financial information in the form of activity costs, product costs, and performance measures. This information serves as a baseline for comparing current process performance against expected results. Such comparisons will help you set improvement targets and justify investments.

THE COMPONENTS OF ABC&P

Exhibit 1-1 is a graphic model of the ABC&P methodology. The circle represents the cost component of ABC&P, and the arrow represents the performance component. This section examines the components of the ABC&P model and explains their roles and relationships. The rest of the book provides specific guidance for how you can apply ABC&P to your organization.

Exhibit 1-1   The ABC&P model incorporates cost and performance.

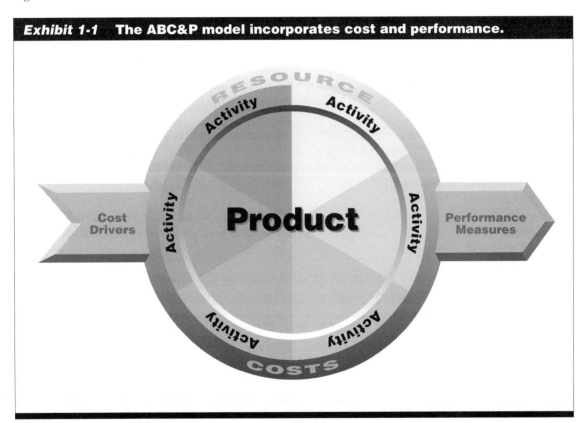

Cost Component

ABC&P assigns the costs of resources to the activities in which they are consumed. Resource costs are shown in the outer ring of Exhibit 1-1; activities are shown in the middle ring. In turn, ABC&P assigns the costs of activities to the products to which they contribute. Products are shown in the center of the circle. In traditional ABC terminology, products are referred to as cost objects. An activity may contribute to one or more products. ABC&P treats products as the end result of a group of activities.

Resource Costs

Resources: the elements (e.g., labor, materials, facilities) used to perform work.

Resources are the elements (e.g., labor, materials and facilities) used to perform work. Because resources cost money to acquire, they are the starting point in the cost measurement process. ABC&P tracks resource costs through the activities that consume them to the cost objects or products that require those activities to be performed. Military personnel, civilian personnel, facilities, supplies, and computer hardware and software are all examples of resources.

Resource Driver: a measure of the consumption of a resource.

Using *resource drivers*, ABC&P assigns the costs of resources used by an activity to that activity. A resource driver is a measure of an activity's resource consumption. It is used to determine the portion of the total cost assigned to each activity that uses the resource. The number of hours a person spends engaging in an activity is an example of a resource driver used to assign the cost of personnel resources to the activity.

Activities

Activity: one step within a process that uses resources to perform work.

An activity is one step within a process that uses resources to perform work. It occurs over time (has a clear beginning and ending) and has recognizable results. Entering data is an activity within the process of preparing a travel voucher. This activity contributes to the end result of a processed travel voucher.

ABC&P helps facilitate BPR efforts by using activities as the focal point for both cost measurement and performance measurement. The cost and performance insights provided by ABC&P will help you concentrate BPR efforts on activities that are heavy resource consumers, as measured by costs, or are heavy contributors of cost drivers to other activities, as measured by performance.

Process: a group of activities performed to achieve a desired business objective(s).

When activities are grouped to achieve a business objective, they are defined as a *process*. One example of this is the process of manufacturing a product on an assembly line. The production process is made up of many individual activities. While BPR focuses on the overall business processes, ABC&P focuses on the individual activities that together compose the processes examined by BPR. In other words, ABC&P provides the breakdown of processes — and the breakdown of cost and performance data — to facilitate BPR.

Activity *drivers* are the mechanisms for assigning the costs of activities to products. An activity driver is a measure of the frequency of activity performance and the effort required to achieve the end result. Take, as an example, training a soldier. When assigning the cost of the activity (teach class) to the product (a trained soldier), the number of classes required is an activity driver. During a BPR exercise you can evaluate whether the cost of the activity is appropriate, given the contribution it makes to the resulting product.

Activity Driver: a measure of the frequency of activity performance and the effort required to achieve the end result.

Products

Refer again to Exhibit 1-1. The ABC&P model shows a *product* as the final point to which costs are assigned. The "product" may actually be a tangible product, a service, a contract, an action, or any other object about which you wish to gain financial and/or non-financial information, through cost and performance measurement. Examples of products are a repaired ship, a trained soldier, a processed travel voucher, or a distribution channel. In traditional ABC terminology, the product is called a cost object. This book uses the term product for simplicity.

Product: any object about which you wish to gain financial or other information through cost and performance measurement.

BPR projects often target specific products for improvement. ABC&P directs BPR efforts toward viewing the product as the result of specific activities, and examining those activities in terms of resource usage and performance. Each activity within a process contributes in some way to the product(s) of that process. This contribution may be direct, in the form of an actual portion of the product, or it may be indirect, in the form of support provided by one activity to other activities. The individual contributions of activities are combined throughout the process to arrive at the desired end result or product.

The cost of a product is based on the resources consumed by the activities performed in producing it. Defining products in terms of activities provides you with a point of reference for determining why activities are performed. It also enables you to distinguish between support activities and activities that directly contribute to the product. Assigning resource costs incurred by support activities to the activities they support helps to accurately account for the cost of consuming these resources.

By costing products, ABC&P also helps measure the impact that changes to individual activities have on the process as a whole. Understanding this impact will help you avoid the problem of making large improvements in individual activities only to realize a minimal improvement to the end result of the whole process.

Performance Component

The performance portion of ABC&P, illustrated by the horizontal arrow in Exhibit 1-1, is made up of cost drivers and performance measures. Cost drivers are factors that influence the level of resources used by an activity, while performance measures reflect the output of the activity. The performance of one activity may become the cost driver of another. In other words, the output of one activity often becomes an input to one or more other activities in the process, as illustrated in **Exhibit 1-2**. Activities can have multiple cost drivers and performance measures.

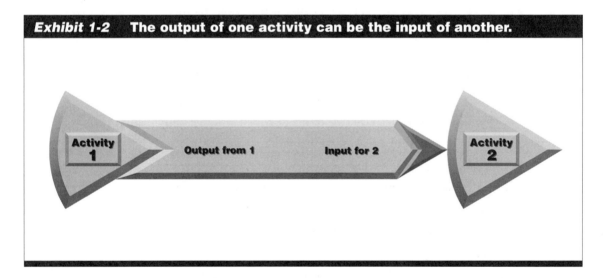

Exhibit 1-2   The output of one activity can be the input of another.

Activity 1 — Output from 1 — Input for 2 — Activity 2

Cost Drivers

Cost Driver: an indicator of why an activity is performed and what causes the cost of performing the activity to change.

Each activity in the ABC&P model has associated *cost drivers*. A cost driver is an indicator, often non-financial, of why an activity is performed and what causes the cost of performing the activity to change. Cost drivers differ from activity drivers in that cost drivers are used to understand what affects the activity's performance. In contrast, activity drivers simply measure the frequency of performance of the activity and the effort required.

An example of a cost driver would be the quality of the input to an activity. If the input is of poor quality, then more effort will be required to make this input usable by the activity that receives it. This adds to the cost of the receiving activity by requiring additional time or steps to be performed, or requiring the entire activity to be performed a second time.

Performance Measures

Each activity has associated *performance measures*. A performance measure is "...an indicator of work performed and the results achieved in an activity. Performance measures communicate how well the activity meets the needs of its internal and external customers and may be financial or non-financial."[1] Information regarding the quality, efficiency, and timeliness of an activity can be gained through the use of performance measures. For example, a performance measure might assess the quality of an activity output by recording the number of errors.

Because the output of one activity can become the input of another activity, the receiving activity's performance is dependent on the supplying activity's output. The receiving activity is the customer of the supplying activity. The performance measures of the supplying activity determine the effort required to perform the receiving activity, and become cost drivers for that activity. This link can be seen in **Exhibit 1-3**.

Performance Measure: an indicator of work performed and the results achieved in an activity.

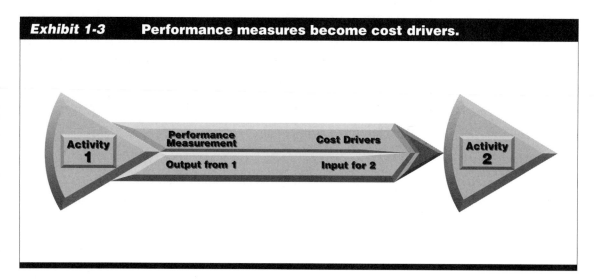

Exhibit 1-3   Performance measures become cost drivers.

---

[1] Turney, Peter B.B.. *Common Cents* (Cost Technology: Hillsboro OR), 1992, p. 88.

ABC&P AND TRADITIONAL COSTING APPROACHES

Traditional accounting approaches collect and report costs by assigning the costs of resources to products. The main premise behind traditional approaches is that products cause costs. Under this assumption, direct resource costs are assigned to the products or services for which they are incurred. Overhead resource costs are spread among products or services based on an allocation scheme. This allocation scheme may or may not reflect actual resource usage. This type of approach focuses on *what* was achieved, the "bottom-line," not on *how* it was achieved.

ABC&P introduces the use of activities as an intermediary for assigning the costs of resources to products. ABC&P is based on the premise that activities cause costs through the consumption of resources, and that the demand for products causes these activities to be performed. This approach provides you with insights into how efficiently and effectively you use resources and how your activities contribute to the costs of your business.

SUMMARY

ABC&P analyzes cost and performance measures to assess the financial and non-financial aspects of an organization's processes. The basic premise of ABC&P is that activities cause costs through their consumption of resources, and that products create a need for performing the activities. ABC&P introduces the concept of using activities to accurately assign the cost of resources to the products that use them. The ABC&P model also includes cost drivers and performance measures for each activity to assess performance and highlight the interdependencies among the activities within a process. The components of the ABC&P model are summarized in **Exhibit 1-4**.

ABC&P Component	Definition	Examples
Resources	The elements (e.g. labor, materials, and facilities) used to perform work	• military & civilian personnel • facilities • supplies • hardware & software
Resource Driver	A measure of the consumption of a resource, used to determine the portion of the total resource cost assigned to each activity that uses the resource	• number of hours to perform the activity • number of square feet occupied • percent of time spent
Activity	One step within a process that uses resources to perform work. It occurs over time and has recognizable results	• test equipment • teach training classes • enter data
Activity Driver	A measure of the frequency of activity performance and the effort required to achieve the end result	• number of classes required • number of forms processed • number of lines of data
Products	Any object that you wish to gain financial and non-financial information about through cost and performance measurement	• repaired ship • trained soldier • processed travel voucher • Army base
Cost Driver	An indicator of why an activity is performed and what causes the cost of performing the activity to change	• proposed work package for a ship • yield rate of the activity • characteristic of a product
Performance Measure	An indicator of the work performed and the results achieved in a activity; a measure of how well an activity meets the needs of its customers	• cycle time • number of errors • customer satisfaction • inventory fill rates

Exhibit 1-4   The ABC&P model consists of several components.

CHAPTER 1

CHAPTER 2

ABC
Performance

Establishing
the Project
Framework

Well begun is half done.

– *ARISTOTLE*

CHAPTER 2: ESTABLISHING THE PROJECT FRAMEWORK

T he first step in applying the concepts of ABC&P to BPR is to establish the project framework. Determine how you will use ABC&P within your BPR effort up front during the following project planning steps:

- Assess the appropriateness of ABC&P for the project
- Gain support from stakeholders
- Evaluate the availability of data and sources
- Define the project approach
- Determine the level of effort required
- Form and train the ABC&P team

ASSESS THE APPROPRIATENESS OF ABC&P FOR THE PROJECT

To realize the benefits of ABC&P, you must be able to document and describe the business process you want to improve in terms of discrete activities that have clear beginnings and endings, produce recognizable results, and consume resources consistently. Consider the following questions for each business process you want to reengineer:

ABC&P may not be appropriate for every project. Thoroughly assess its appropriateness before you begin.

- Is the process repeatable?
- Can it be defined by a discrete set of activities?
- Can you define the customers' expectations?
- Can you collect the data necessary to analyze the process within your time and resource constraints?

If the answer to any of these questions is no, ABC&P is not an appropriate tool for this particular project. If the answer to all these questions is yes, continue the process of establishing your project framework.

ASSESS THE APPROPRIATENESS OF ABC&P

TelAmerica is a regional telephone company. It is divided into several divisions, including a Telecommunications Device Division. TelAmerica analyzed the Telecommunications Device Division to target areas of improvement. They determined that an overall 10% cost reduction would be possible. The division managers passed this figure down as the goal for their Telephone Repair Facility to meet.

The facility repairs TelAmerica's full range of telephones, consisting of 40 telephones of varying complexity. The customer base includes individual end users, retailers and corporate end users. All customers are concerned with getting their telephones properly repaired within a reasonable amount of time. Chris Hill, the General Manager of the facility, is excited at the opportunity to reengineer. She wants to use ABC&P to determine how to make the necessary changes to her business processes, and cut costs without negatively affecting customer service.

GAIN SUPPORT FROM STAKEHOLDERS

Support from stakeholders is vital to your project's success.

Support from key individuals, or stakeholders, is essential to your project's success. Stakeholders are the people and organizations who have a vested interest in the project and can influence its outcome. Failure to gain support from stakeholders will likely cause your project to fail. Identify these people and organizations at the beginning of the project and review their opinion of the project periodically throughout the course of the project. Typical key stakeholders are project sponsors, process participants, process customers, and financial, data processing, and administrative staff. After identifying the stakeholders, determine their interests and objectives, then develop a plan for dealing with their interests. Work with stakeholders to help them understand what the project is trying to accomplish and how it will benefit them. Instill ownership by keeping them informed of the progress and accomplishments. As an extra measure, assign a project member to work with stakeholders individually to help manage their expectations.

EVALUATE THE AVAILABILITY OF DATA AND SOURCES

Accurate and useful data is critical to the success of ABC&P and BPR, and obtaining it will be a challenging aspect of your BPR effort. Determine whether or not the data you need is available, and whether or not it is accurate. Then, determine where to get additional data and how much effort will be involved in collecting it. Often, data will not be readily available or recognizable because most systems do not track information at the activity level. Costs are generally reported by organizational element, appropriation category, or other schemes to meet minimum reporting requirements. In DoD, for example, costs may be reported differently by each military component and may also be reported differently within a single organization. Assess sources that are not worth the effort to examine, and those that will help in the effort.

Evaluate potential data sources and select the appropriate collection method.

There are four primary methods for collecting data for your BPR effort:

- Documentation
- Interviews
- Questionnaires
- Workshops

Keep in mind that these methods are not mutually exclusive. You can interview people to determine what reports are available, conduct a workshop with key people and validate the results of an interview, or distribute a questionnaire and review it in an interview. It is important to select the technique or combination of techniques that works best given the type of information you need to collect, the sources of that information, the availability of the people that have the information, the resources available, and the reliability of the data.

Documentation

Documentation, in either hard copy or electronic form, provides a good source of data. Enhance the value of data from documentation with interviews and additional fact finding. Always verify the accuracy of the data before accepting it. Find out how the data in a report was generated. Who uses it? What was its original source? How valid is the source? What is the likelihood of data entry errors? What was done to the data once it entered the system?

Interviews

Interviewing is time-consuming, but it provides immediate confirmation and allows you to easily clarify results. Interviewing is a good technique to use when collecting relatively small amounts of data or subjective or complex data that requires detailed explanations. It is important to select the appropriate people to interview. Set the context for the interview by explaining the purpose of the interview to the interviewee, why his or her help is needed, and how the information will be used once it is provided. Prepare a list of questions and give it to the interviewee in advance so he or she is prepared. Keep the interview focused on these questions.

Do not overwhelm the interviewee with too many people. Have one person lead the discussion and a second person take notes. Document the results of the interview immediately (or as soon as possible) after the interview. This is an extremely important step that must be planned into the interview schedule. Too often, valuable information gathered during the interview process is lost because the interview team did not take the time to document the results. Finally, ensure that the interview notes and documentation are organized so that the needed information is readily available.

Questionnaires

Questionnaires are useful when collecting large quantities of data from many sources. Use questionnaires to obtain information about data that is readily available to the people filling out the form. If they have to go through a great deal of effort (e.g., perform calculations) to complete the form, they are less likely to respond, and the quality of the data will be questionable.

To make effective use of questionnaires, ensure that the questions are clear, unambiguous, and easy to answer. If possible, assign a point person at each site who understands the purpose of the questionnaire and can help collect the information. Allow adequate time for people to complete the questionnaire and provide a mechanism (names and corresponding telephone numbers) for asking follow-up questions if necessary. Consider using forms that can be read by optical character readers or scanners so that the results can be quickly entered into a database for analysis.

Workshops

Workshops are an excellent means for collecting data when group consensus or input is required (e.g., activity modeling). The advantage of a workshop is that multiple perspectives can be discussed and analyzed at once. The disadvantages are that it may be difficult to get the appropriate people together for the necessary length of time, and it can be difficult to reach consensus.

To use workshops effectively, plan them in advance. Know exactly what you need to accomplish and how to accomplish it. It may take as long or longer to plan the workshop as it will to conduct it. Make sure the workshop attendees are prepared by giving them a briefing package to read in advance. Use experienced facilitators to plan and run the session. It takes an experienced, unbiased facilitator, with training in group dynamics and group management techniques, to create the open atmosphere required for a productive, effective workshop. Consider electronic meeting software as a mechanism to keep workshops focused, and provide ample opportunity for everyone to voice his or her thoughts.

Other Alternatives

If needed data is not available, recognize that the insights into the current problems will be more subjective and possibly less credible. Assess the impact of the lack of accurate data and choose one of three options: (1) cancel the project, if the value to be gained is not worth the cost of the effort; (2) delay the project until mechanisms can be established to collect the necessary data; (3) continue the project on schedule, if other information is available that might add value to the BPR initiative. Are there credible, reliable experts who understand the problem? Can useful insights from the project still be gained? Will the necessary support from the sponsor, functional and financial communities still be forthcoming?

DEFINE THE PROJECT APPROACH

Define an ABC&P project approach that is consistent with your BPR approach.

Your approach for performing ABC&P modeling and analysis must consider and be consistent with the purpose of your BPR project, the nature and size of the problem, the availability of data, and time and resource constraints. Your approach for your BPR project will provide natural boundaries and will serve to focus the ABC&P modeling and analysis. Identify the following to define your project approach:

- Purpose
- Objectives
- Scope
- Major phases/tasks
- Schedule for completing phases/tasks

Purpose

In a short purpose statement, reflect the motivation for initiating the project and what you wish to achieve. Also specify how you will use ABC&P to accomplish the BPR effort.

Objectives

Objectives are specific things you must do to achieve the purpose. Carefully list all the objectives that support your purpose. If you satisfy all the objectives, you will achieve your purpose. Your objectives should reflect ambitious but realistic targets.

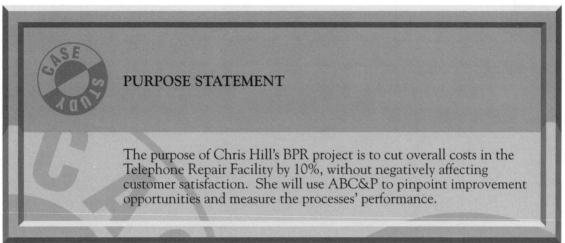

PURPOSE STATEMENT

The purpose of Chris Hill's BPR project is to cut overall costs in the Telephone Repair Facility by 10%, without negatively affecting customer satisfaction. She will use ABC&P to pinpoint improvement opportunities and measure the processes' performance.

Scope

The scope defines the boundaries of what to include in your project, and helps keep your team focused. Your BPR project scope should adequately address all of the issues needed to satisfy the BPR purpose and objectives, given time and budget constraints. Include a description of the processes to be evaluated for change, their context within the business enterprise, and the resources that can be committed to the project. In the scope of the ABC&P project, define the degree to which processes should be modeled. This includes both deciding which activities need to be included and making a preliminary decision regarding the level of breakdown required.

Major Phases/Tasks

Develop a hierarchical definition of tasks to identify the major tasks you need to perform to complete your project, and the time each task will require. The highest level of the definition should include the major phases of the project. For example, the major phases for a project to improve business practices in an organization that performs the same process differently at multiple sites would be as follows:

1. Develop a generic activity model for all sites to the lowest level possible.
2. Develop a generic ABC&P model (framework) that represents most sites.
3. Add site-unique aspects if these aspects have a significant impact.
4. Collect data and assign values to the ABC&P model for each site.
5. Compare cost and performance across sites to identify a new standard process.

6. Transition to the new baseline.

7. Identify opportunities for more significant improvements and implement these changes.

Break down each of these phases further into subtasks. It is often useful to think in terms of the interim products that are going to be created on the way to achieving the end result.

DEFINE OBJECTIVES AND MAJOR TASKS

Chris identified four objectives and the tasks required to accomplish them.

Objective One: <u>Understand the status quo from an activity and cost perspective</u>. Meeting this objective will require developing an As-Is activity model and ABC&P model.

Objective Two: <u>Identify what the problem areas are in the current business practice</u>. Attaining this objective will involve using various analysis techniques to isolate improvement opportunities.

Objective Three: <u>Create an alternative business practice addressing as many of the improvement opportunities as possible</u>. This will require conducting brainstorming sessions of possible alternatives and selecting one for implementation.

Objective Four: <u>Develop an implementation plan for the new business practice and implement it</u>. This will require developing a transition plan of the new practice, training selected staff members in how to implement it, and offering support services as those staff implement it on the repair line.

Schedule Constraints

You must execute the project on time and within budget. Develop rough estimates of key resources (e.g., employees, consultants, equipment, facilities, and automated tools) needed to complete the project in the allotted time.

Maintaining project focus is critical to keeping the BPR effort on schedule. Many people spend months analyzing the current business practices, only to run out of time and money to design new business practices. There are two reasons it is easy to fall into this trap:

- It is difficult to reach consensus on how the current business processes work.
- It is easier for people to deal with today (the As-Is) than to design the future processes (the To-Be).

Avoid "paralysis by analysis" by remaining focused on the purpose, objectives, and scope defined for the project.

DETERMINE THE LEVEL OF EFFORT REQUIRED

The level of effort required for a project is driven by the project scope, resources available for completion, and the planned approach. It also depends on the skill and experience of the project team and the amount of time allotted to complete the project. The more detailed the analysis, the greater the required level of effort.

ABC&P is useful for a full range of effort levels.

ABC&P can cover a wide spectrum of effort levels from "back of the envelope" analysis to detailed activity models. Define activities to a level that will be effective in terms of your BPR effort, but not to a level where the modeling portion becomes a project in itself. By focusing on the objectives of BPR, you will more easily calibrate the ABC&P effort with your desired results. **Exhibit 2-1** illustrates factors that influence the level of effort involved in performing ABC&P to support BPR.

FORM AND TRAIN THE ABC&P TEAM

A team is a group of people with complementary skills who share a common purpose, work toward the same performance goals, and follow the same work approach for which they hold each other mutually accountable.[1]

Effective ABC&P teams consist of people with a variety of backgrounds.

[1] Katzenback, Jon R. & Douglas K. Smith. *The Wisdom of Teams* (Harvard Business Press: Boston, MA), 1993, p. 45.

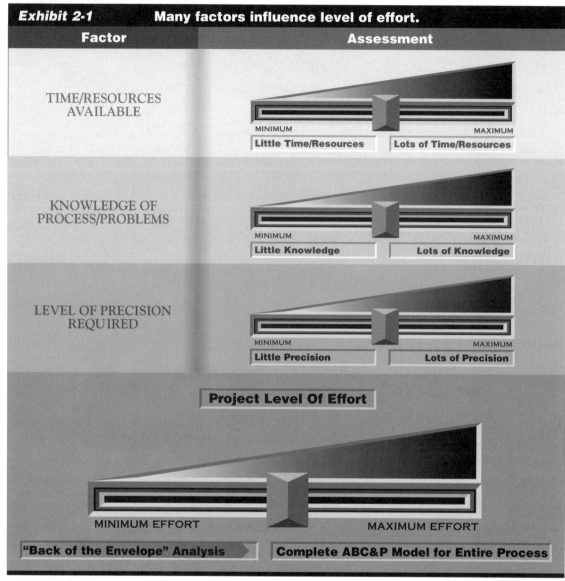

Exhibit 2-1   **Many factors influence level of effort.**

Factor	Assessment
TIME/RESOURCES AVAILABLE	MINIMUM — MAXIMUM / Little Time/Resources — Lots of Time/Resources
KNOWLEDGE OF PROCESS/PROBLEMS	MINIMUM — MAXIMUM / Little Knowledge — Lots of Knowledge
LEVEL OF PRECISION REQUIRED	MINIMUM — MAXIMUM / Little Precision — Lots of Precision

Project Level Of Effort

MINIMUM EFFORT — MAXIMUM EFFORT

"Back of the Envelope" Analysis — Complete ABC&P Model for Entire Process

A good analysis team consists of a mix of people, some of whom are intimately familiar with the processes (subject matter experts), and others who are experienced in analyzing business problems and understanding how to apply the various tools and techniques. Your ABC&P analysis team should be trained in the use of modeling techniques, analysis techniques, automated tools, and team-building skills.

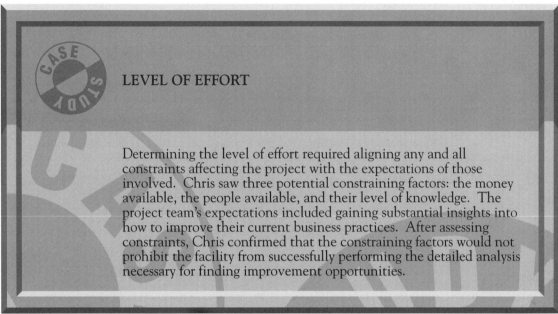

LEVEL OF EFFORT

Determining the level of effort required aligning any and all constraints affecting the project with the expectations of those involved. Chris saw three potential constraining factors: the money available, the people available, and their level of knowledge. The project team's expectations included gaining substantial insights into how to improve their current business practices. After assessing constraints, Chris confirmed that the constraining factors would not prohibit the facility from successfully performing the detailed analysis necessary for finding improvement opportunities.

You should consider supplementing the analysis team with people who play the following roles:

- *Technology Expert* – understands and can assess the impact of technology on the processes being reengineered.
- *Change Agent* – Leads and facilitates change within the organization.
- *Facilitator* – leads workshops for developing the models and collecting the data. The facilitator is an unbiased person who ensures that all workshop participants have a chance to discuss their ideas in meetings. This person remains neutral in discussions with other meeting members.
- *Administrative support* – maintains databases, iterations of models, meeting minutes, libraries, etc.

No single team structure will work for every project. Your team must be structured to suit your particular approach. Also, the organizational structure for your project team need not be static. As the project progresses through the various phases, people may move among different teams and may take on different roles as appropriate. For example, single-function teams may develop the As-Is model and then cross-functional teams may develop To-Be models of different alternatives. The level of involvement and the roles of team members will change as the project progresses through its phases.

Teamwork is critical to the success of the project. It takes a concentrated effort to turn a group of people into a good team. A team with complementary skills, a common purpose, a common approach, and mutual accountability achieves greater results than the individuals working alone. Effective leadership is also critical. A good leader provides the motivation and inspiration for a group that is necessary to facilitate teamwork and maintain a group's efforts in a direction consistent with a common mission.

SUMMARY

Before performing ABC&P, you must complete the following preliminary steps: assess the appropriateness of ABC&P for the BPR project, gain critical support for the project, evaluate the availability of data and sources, define the project approach, determine the level of effort required to carry it out, and form and train the team. These steps will help you effectively integrate ABC&P into your BPR project and will provide the project framework — the boundaries in which to apply ABC&P modeling and analysis.

CHAPTER 1
CHAPTER 2
CHAPTER 3

ABC&
Performance

Establishing
the ABC&P
Baseline

He who knows others is wise.
He who knows himself is enlightened.

– LAO-TZU

CHAPTER 3: ESTABLISHING THE ABC&P BASELINE

Improving the way your organization does business through BPR requires that you first understand the performance and cost effectiveness of your current way of doing business. This chapter discusses how to model your As-Is process. The chapter starts with an overview of activity modeling and then covers the five steps involved in establishing the ABC&P baseline:

- Develop the As-Is activity model
- Identify all ABC&P components
- Collect data
- Calculate activity costs
- Calculate product costs

UNDERSTAND ACTIVITY MODEL BASICS

An activity model is a graphic representation of the activities that compose a business process. An activity model also shows the flow of information and objects (e.g., forms, reports, products) used and created by these activities, and the resources consumed by the activities (e.g., labor,

An activity model is a graphic representation of the activities that compose a business process, the flow of information and objects used and created by these activities, and the resources consumed by the activities.

facilities, materials, equipment, technology). For a BPR effort, each activity in the activity model must have a clear beginning and end, it must produce recognizable results (a single output that is measurable and contributes to the product), and it must consume resources consistently each time it is performed.

A Useful Activity Model

A *useful* activity model is one that provides all information needed for the analysis in a structure that does not require many new calculations or reshuffling of data. It is accurate, complete, and understandable.

An *accurate* model is one that reflects reality. An accurate As-Is model reflects how work is currently done. A *complete* model covers all of the activities, resources, products, and relationships that are relevant to the analysis.

An *understandable* model can be easily interpreted and used by people that are not involved in the modeling effort, but who are familiar with the processes. Also, it enables people to envision the way work is actually accomplished. Models are tools for communicating and performing analysis. If people cannot understand the model, they cannot tell if it accurately reflects reality, and they cannot provide the data needed to perform the analysis (e.g., resource consumption rates, frequency, duration).

The Need for an Activity Model

Activity modeling is the mechanism for defining, organizing, and communicating the activity piece of the ABC&P model. One approach to activity modeling is establishing a hierarchical list of activities. This approach is not adequate for ABC&P. Hierarchical lists do not show how activities interact or the dependencies among the activities. This information helps ensure that there is a complete and accurate portrayal of a current process, and helps identify problems with that process. Furthermore, a simple hierarchical list of activities does not link activities with resources or products. Because the linking of activities is needed to support your ABC&P effort, these relationships must be depicted in your activity model.

Designing an Activity Model

Several different modeling techniques address the limitations of hierarchical activity lists. This book uses the (Integrated Definition Methodology, Zero) IDEF0[1] modeling technique, developed by the Air Force. The Department of Defense Corporate Information Management (CIM) Information Technology Policy Board has adopted IDEF0 as the mandatory technique for modeling business processes. A brief introduction to IDEF0 modeling is provided here. For additional information about IDEF0, see the further readings list in the back of the book.

Exhibit 3-1 shows the basic components of an IDEF0 model. The process, or activity, is represented in the box. The arrows coming into the left side of the box represent *inputs*. Inputs are things that are acted upon or transformed by the process. The arrows coming out of the right side of the box are the *outputs* of the process. Outputs are products or services. The arrows coming in from the bottom of the chart are the *mechanisms* that help perform the activity. The arrows coming in from the top of the box are the *controls*. Controls are those things that constrain the process.

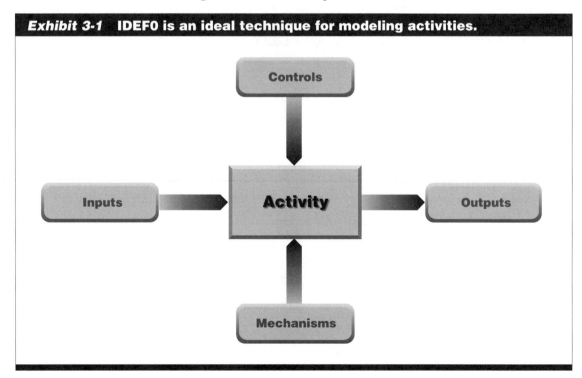

Exhibit 3-1 **IDEF0 is an ideal technique for modeling activities.**

Controls

Inputs

Activity

Outputs

Mechanisms

---

[1] IDEF0 is pronounced, "eye deaf zero."

Many BPR and ABC&P efforts focus on relatively complex business processes. A model of a complex business process will typically include several layers or levels, arranged in a hierarchy where the top-most activity (level 0) represents the business process. This top-most activity is subdivided into the activities contained in level 1. Level 1 activities are then further subdivided into the activities in level 2, and so on, as illustrated in **Exhibit 3-2**. This hierarchical structure is a node tree. The next section provides you with practical guidance on how to organize and structure your As-Is activity model.

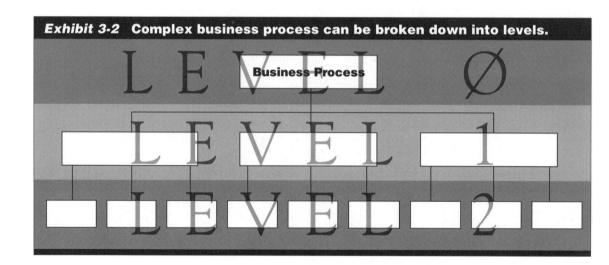

Exhibit 3-2 Complex business process can be broken down into levels.

DEVELOP THE AS-IS ACTIVITY MODEL

Some modeling experts advocate a strict top-down approach, starting at the top of the hierarchy with the business process, decomposing it into its parts, and continuing in this top-down fashion until reaching the bottom. Others say that a bottom-up approach is better, starting by listing all of the detailed steps performed and grouping them into categories. Using a combination of the two approaches will work best for developing your As-Is model.

Starting at the top will help you get a clear understanding of the scope of the process being modeled. Take a first-cut at defining the level 1 activities by breaking the business process into its logical components. If studying a very complex process, take a first-cut at the level 2 activities, but do not go too far with the top-down approach, and do not spend too much time agonizing over these "first-cut" models because they will undoubtedly change. These high level activity models should reflect an end-to-end view of your business where each process starts with a demand for a product and ends with that product being delivered to the customer. When building the activity model, concentrate on *what* work is done and *how* it is done, not *who* does the work.

Now start the bottom-up approach. List all of the activities people spend time doing. Talk to people either through interviews or workshops to gain an appreciation of how these people spend their time. Direct observation of people as they work may also help define the activities that are performed.

Once you have developed this list of activities, review and refine the list until it is complete, accurate, and usable. Then allocate the activities in the list to the "first-cut" level 1 activity model developed earlier. Logical groupings will become obvious. Keep track of these, as they will become the levels in the model. If the "first-cut" level 1 groupings of activities are not working well (e.g., if 80 percent of the activities are allocated to a single level 1 activity and the remaining 20 percent are spread among four or five level 1 activities) consider redefining the level 1 activities. Remember that this is an iterative process, and there is no single right answer.

When identifying activities, it is important to consider the nature of the input that triggers the activity. Some activities are triggered by a single product for a customer (one unit), and their costs are directly proportional to the level of production. Others are triggered by batches or groups of products. For example, setup, material movement, and planning are incurred every time a batch of products is processed, regardless of the volume of production. Still others, such as facility maintenance, are required simply to sustain the organization.

It is also important that an activity have only a single output. This restriction is necessary to accurately cost products. Frequently, a single activity appears to have two or more outputs. This problem can be resolved by either further decomposing the activity until an activity has been defined for each output, or leaving the activity at the current level and combining the outputs into a single output.

For example, an activity model of a military finance office might include as one of its activities "Dispense Funds to Military Personnel." The outputs, determined by interviewing the cashier, are identified as "Military Payroll Checks" and "Military Travel and Moving Pay." Because ABC&P requires a single output per activity, the activity "Dispense Funds to Military Personnel" could be further subdivided into "Dispense Payroll to Military Personnel," and "Dispense Travel and Moving Pay to Military Personnel." The alternative solution would be to combine the outputs into the single output "Military Pay (Payroll/Travel/Moving)." The choice is dependent on the level of analysis needed to support the purpose, and the cost versus the value of additional decomposition.

It is important to develop the As-Is model so that other people can understand it. Keep giving the As-Is model an "audience perspective check." Will the people providing the data for this model understand what a given activity means? Will they be able to provide good, reliable information about how much time they spend performing the activity, what resources are used to perform the activity, etc.? If the answer to either question is no, redefine the activities to make them understandable.

Modeling is never complete. Many people often wonder to what level of detail they need to take their analysis. The answer is, "it depends." It depends on how much information is needed to achieve the objectives. Each time you add another level of detail to an activity model, you significantly increase your workload with respect to collecting and analyzing data. It is important to stay focused on the objectives and the required data. Modeling is a tool rather than an end objective. Therefore, the depth of your analysis should be consistent with the amount of information you need to improve decision-making. High cost or high leverage activities provide the best opportunities for improvement and should therefore be analyzed in more detail than low cost or low leverage activities. All activities do not need to be defined to the same level of detail.

IDENTIFY ALL ABC&P COMPONENTS

The next step in establishing the baseline is identifying all of the necessary components of the ABC&P model. Activity models form the foundation for designing and implementing ABC&P models. This relationship makes identifying ABC&P components easier. Because IDEF0 is the modeling approach recommended for use by DoD, references to the

DEVELOPING AN ACTIVITY MODEL

Chris interviewed the people responsible for each major activity to establish preliminary activity models. She validated the final model in a workshop. The activity model contained the following activities (levels are shown by indentation):

Repair Telephone
- Receive Telephones
  - Record Customer Information (Walk-In)
  - Record Customer Information (Mail/Dock)
  - Record Problem Information (Walk-In)
  - Record Problem Information (Mail/Dock)
- Move Internally
  - Forward Repair Order to Data Processing
  - Forward Telephone with Repair Order to Testing Station
  - Forward to Shipping
- Track Repair Orders
  - Enter Repair Order
  - Record Shipment
- Test Telephones
  - Test Low Complexity Phones
  - Test High Complexity Phones
- Prepare Technical Documents
- Repair and Replace
- Pack Telephones for Shipping
  - Package Lots (Walk-In)
  - Package Units (Walk-In)
  - Package Lots (Mail/Dock)
  - Package Units (Mail/Dock)
- Ship Telephones

activity model in this book assume the use of IDEF0 for activity modeling. However, the concepts remain valid regardless of the modeling approach you take. **Exhibit 3-3** summarizes the relationships between IDEF0 components and the products, activities, and resources you need to identify for your ABC&P model.

Exhibit 3-3 IDEF0 and ABC&P model components are related.	
IDEF0 Component	**ABC&P Component**
Activity	Activities
Controls	Activities only when the cost of the activity performed to generate the control is significant and when the activity is performed within the parent organization
Inputs	Resources only when provided by sources external to the process
Mechanisms	Resources
Outputs	Products (one product may comprise several outputs)

Product(s)

As you gather information about ABC&P components, organize it into a database.

Define an output for each activity as part of the activity modeling exercise. Generally, the products for which you will calculate costs come from this group of outputs. At the highest levels, you can intuitively choose products to cost based on knowledge of the business and the customers of the process. At this high level, the defined products may consist of several outputs. At lower levels, the products to be costed become evident based on what information is needed for analysis. As you gather product related information (activities, activity drivers, activity driver values), organize and store it in a product database.

The definition of products varies in type and level of detail. Product hierarchies represent these different levels of detail (**Exhibit 3-4**). The ability to define products at different levels enables ABC&P to be relevant at different organizational levels (e.g. from logistics command headquarters to the shop floor of a depot). The key to taking full advantage of product costing under ABC&P is to understand the flexibility of ABC&P in determining the cost of various products, and then use that flexibility to provide the data most helpful to decision-makers. To obtain useful financial and non-financial performance information, define products in a manner and level of detail consistent with the purpose and objectives of the project.

Assigning costs to lower-level products can provide important insights unavailable at higher levels. If, for example, parts differ in design complex-

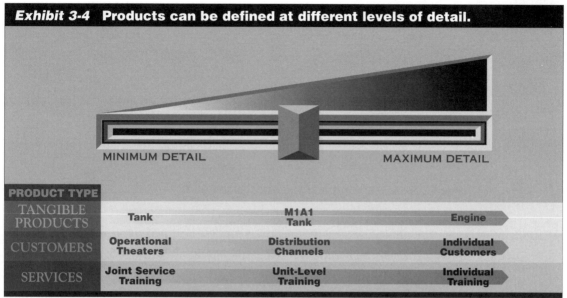

Exhibit 3-4 Products can be defined at different levels of detail.

MINIMUM DETAIL		MAXIMUM DETAIL

PRODUCT TYPE			
TANGIBLE PRODUCTS	Tank	M1A1 Tank	Engine
CUSTOMERS	Operational Theaters	Distribution Channels	Individual Customers
SERVICES	Joint Service Training	Unit-Level Training	Individual Training

ity or production volume, ABC&P can cost those parts so that sourcing decisions can be made at the part level. This allows depot managers to make a more informed decision of whether to repair a part internally, or to use an outside vendor. This also provides insight for making product and process design tradeoff decisions, which can be helpful for implementing concurrent engineering[2] or similar undertakings.

Activities

The activities costed in the ABC&P analysis come from the activities included in the activity model. You may not need to cost activities to the same level of detail you modeled them; however, all activities you cost should be included in the activity model. Once again, analyze to the level from which you will gain valuable insights. This level varies from project to project. As you gather activity information (resources, resource drivers, cost drivers, performance measures), organize and store it in an activity database.

Perform analysis only to the level from which you will gain valuable insights.

The controls included in the IDEF0 activity model are the output of some activity or group of activities that consume resources in the generation of those controls. The cost of the activities that generate the controls may

---

[2] Concurrent engineering is the simultaneous and integrated development of products and their associated processes.

or may not be relevant to your particular ABC&P effort. To assess which of these activities to include in your ABC&P model, consider who is responsible for these activities and the expected costs of the activities.

First consider the controls generated by activities performed within your parent organization[3]. If the expected cost of the activities performed to generate these controls is significant, the costs of these activities need to be included in your analysis. The danger of not including the costs of these activities is that you may identify sub-optimal solutions that do not consider the costs of internally generated controls.

Activities performed within your parent organization may or may not be included in the current activity model. If an activity is already included in the activity model, including this activity in the ABC&P model will allow you to account for the cost of generating the control. The cost of generating the control will be accounted for in the cost calculated for the activity. If, however, a control is generated by an activity that is not currently included in the activity model, you need to make a decision to either (1) include the activity in question in the activity model and ABC&P model, or (2) identify the inaccuracies of the resulting activity costs and accept them.

Some of these activities may be within the control of your parent organization but outside the control of your project sponsor. If such an activity is included in your activity and ABC&P models, recognize that you may not be able to change that activity. You may instead only be able to present the activity cost for generating the control and recommend changes to the control or activity.

Controls may also be generated by activities performed by organizations outside of your parent organization. For example, procurement laws generated by Congress may be controls on a DoD acquisition process. The cost of the activities responsible for generating these controls is not relevant to your analysis because you have little or no influence over the activities and the associated costs. Therefore, do not include such activities in your activity or ABC&P models.

---

[3] A parent organization is the organizational entity that spans the process(es) under analysis. The parent organization and the processes being modeled are often not the same.

Resources

A relationship exists between the mechanisms and inputs defined in the IDEF0 activity model and the resources identified for the ABC&P Model. For ABC&P analysis, *mechanisms* are synonymous with the *resources* consumed by the activity. Mechanisms are defined as resources that "...provide energy to, or perform the activity."[4] The manpower, utilities, facilities, etc. necessary to perform the activity in question typically fall into this category.

Inputs may or may not indicate resource consumption. An input indicates resource consumption only when it is supplied by a source external to the process, such as a vendor. For example, raw materials purchased from an outside vendor are identified as resources to include in the ABC&P model. An input received from another activity within the process is not considered a resource. The costs associated with that input have already been accounted for in the cost of the supplying activity.

The transformation of an input into an output may result in the generation of scrap material. The cost implications of scrap may be significant and may need to be identified to improve the process. In this case, the scrap generated by an activity could be considered to be a resource consumed by the activity.

Resource and Activity Drivers

Resource drivers measure the consumption of resources by activities and are used to assign resource costs to activities. Similarly, activity drivers measure the volume and level of effort required of activities by products and are the means of assigning the cost of activity usage to products. Activities cause the consumption of resources and products cause activities to be performed. If you can identify resource drivers and activity drivers, you can accurately determine activity and product costs.

You can assign costs to activities and products in two ways: tracing and allocation. *Tracing* assigns resource costs to activities and activity costs to products based on an observable measure of the resources consumed or the activities performed. The measure chosen should reasonably reflect what causes the resource consumption by the activity or the activity usage by the

Tracing: The assignment of resource costs to activities and activity costs to products based on an observable measure of the resources consumed or the activities performed.

---

[4] Appleton, D. Company, Inc. *Corporate Information Management Process Improvement Methodology For DoD Functional Managers*, (Fairfax, VA), 1987, p. 66.

Allocation: The assignment of resource costs to activities or activity costs to products through apportionment or distribution. It is used when a direct measure of resource consumption or activity usage does not exist.

product. *Allocation* assigns resource costs to activities or activity costs to products through apportionment or distribution. Allocation is used when a direct measure of resource consumption or activity usage does not exist.

The degree to which you can establish a causal relationship depends on the particular resource and activity in question. It is very likely that assigning costs to activities and activities to products will entail some degree of subjectivity. The degree of subjectivity involved in assigning costs to activities varies from case to case, and determines whether costs can be traced, or must be allocated. Your goal is to assign costs in the most objective manner practical. This will ensure that activity and product costs are more easily understood and less subject to debate.

Whenever possible and practical, trace costs to the activities and products that consume those costs. Tracing costs to activities and activities to products provides much of the power of ABC&P. Tracing establishes a more causal relationship between resource consumption and the activities that benefit, and between activity usage and the products that benefit.

For example, if you are assigning the cost of electric power to an activity, you may be able to use the number of kilowatt hours used by each activity, if available. A kilowatt hour is a direct measure of the consumption of electricity. You could then define the resource driver for electricity as the number of kilowatt hours and use it to trace the cost of electricity to each activity.

There may be situations when tracing costs is not practical. Government cost systems often do not measure costs by activity, especially indirect costs. It may be possible to trace these costs, but is not practical to do so. These situations include the following when:

- Resources or activities are shared in a manner not clearly defined or measured
- Measurement is impractical or costly
- Measurement lacks materiality (insufficient value for cost incurred)

In these situations, you may need to use allocation. When allocation is necessary, use it in a manner that minimizes arbitrariness.

In the previous example, suppose that instead of the number of kilowatt hours, only the number of machine hours used by each activity is available.

Unless all activities use machines with the same kilowatt-hour ratings, machine hours are not a direct measure of electricity usage. In this case, you may allocate the cost of electricity to activities according to the percentage of total machine hours used by each activity. Machine hours become a substitute measure for kilowatt-hours. Such a substitute measure has accuracy limitations. The limitations may be acceptable, however, given the cost of measuring electric power directly.

You can sometimes convert from allocation to tracing by incurring additional measurement charges. For example, your accounting system may only capture electrical power costs for the entire facility. However, you could install watt meters on electrically operated machines to trace electrical power consumption to specific activities.

The difference between tracing and allocation is not always clearly definable. For example, if all electricity is consumed by machines having the exact same wattage, machine hours might be just as accurate as measuring electricity consumed within each activity by placing watt meters on each machine. However, if the machines vary greatly in power requirements, machine hours could become an almost meaningless measure. Good ABC&P analysis is not about the labels of tracing and allocation, but instead it is about applying measures in as meaningfully a manner as practical.

Considerations in Driver Selection

An ideal resource or activity driver accomplishes several things at once. Consider the following in selecting good resource and activity drivers:

- *Accuracy*: The driver closely correlates to resource consumption or activity usage during normal operations.
- *Behavioral Influence*: The driver encourages management actions that are aligned with overall corporate goals.
- *Ease of Measuring*: The driver is easily measured and interpreted.
- *Predictability*: The driver has a correlation with resource consumption that is relatively insensitive to production volume.
- *Availability of Data*: Data about the driver is currently being collected.

Activity Driver Hierarchy

Activity drivers have a hierarchy that corresponds to the nature of the input triggering the activity. Recall that some activities are triggered by a single product (one unit), while others are triggered by batches or groups of products. When defining activity drivers, avoid using the same activity driver for activities triggered by different types of inputs. For example, it might be tempting to combine setup activities with unit production activities, and then assign these combined costs through a unit-level activity driver. However, setup is a batch-level activity, and batch-level costs vary with the number of batches, not with the number of units produced. Assigning batch-level costs with a unit-level driver results in the allocation of costs, rather than the tracing of costs on a causal basis. While this would save some time, it would cloud insight into the sources of the activity costs and would introduce the distortion of reported product costs found in traditional cost systems. The different levels of activities and activity drivers and examples of associated activities are shown in **Exhibit 3-5.**

Exhibit 3-5	Activities drivers have a hierarchy.	
Level of Activity Driver	**Description**	**Example of Activities**
Unit Volume	Performed every time a unit is produced	– Drilling a hole – Supplying electricity
Batch-Related	Performed every time a batch is produced	– Setting up a machine – Moving a batch – Ordering a purchased part
Product-Sustaining	Performed to enable a product to be produced	– Engineering a product – Marketing a product
Technology-Sustaining	Performed to enable a technology to produce a product	– Maintaining a machine – Attending a course
Customer-Sustaining	Performed to service customers and prospects	– Delivering a product – Resolving complaints
Facility-Sustaining	Performed to enable production to occur	– Lighting the factory

Cost Drivers

Identifying appropriate cost drivers for activities is often more of an art than a science. While the following general guidelines are useful, identifying possible cost drivers frequently requires insight and ingenuity.

Cost drivers are associated with the inputs of activities. They should reflect what causes an activity to be performed and what causes the cost of performing the activity to change. Choose cost drivers that reflect prior activity performance and internal process factors. An example of an important cost driver to consider is the expected yield of each activity within the process. The yield rate is the amount of usable output expressed as a percentage of the input. For example, when entering data for a travel

IDENTIFYING ALL ABC&P COMPONENTS

After developing an activity model, Chris identified the components of her ABC&P model. Identifying some components was easy. She already identified her activities when she developed her activity model. She knew she could identify her resources later when collecting her data. Now she needed to identify her product.

Identifying a product was not as easy as Chris originally thought it would be. Because she does not make telephones, her product is not a telephone. Chris provides a service that adds value to a telephone going through her facility. She changes a broken telephone into a repaired telephone. She determined her product to be a repaired telephone.

Confident her data would be free from random fluctuations (growth spurts, etc.), Chris decided the time period for the study (last month) and started identifying her activity drivers. To do this, she asked herself two questions: how often was each activity performed and what measure describes how often each activity was performed. As an example, for the activity "Record Customer Information (Walk-In)," her database showed that 2500 customers personally brought their telephones to the facility last month. This activity driver's volume is therefore 2500. This data came from the number of repair orders (ROs). The number of ROs is the activity driver. Chris continued this process for the rest of the activities.

Chris then defined the resource driver component. This information was readily available. To calculate the resource driver for the facilities/utilities resource costs, for example, she needed only to know how much space the activity occupied.

order, if 10% of the data is incorrect and needs to be reentered, the yield rate for the activity "Enter Data" is 90%. A higher yield rate would decrease the amount of work necessary to produce the required output, thereby lowering costs.

A specific characteristic of a product can be identified as a cost driver if it causes activities to be performed. For example, a sunroof on a car may be considered a cost driver. Only if the customer orders the sunroof option for the car will it be necessary to perform the activities associated with installing a sunroof.

The cost drivers you define should be the most influential factors that drive activity performance. The considerations listed previously for choosing resource and activity drivers are also applicable for choosing cost drivers. **Exhibit 3-6** illustrates one approach for identifying cost drivers as well as resource and activity drivers. This example illustrates the complexity that may be involved in identifying drivers.

Performance Measures

Quantity, quality, timeliness, and customer satisfaction are good things to keep in mind when choosing performance measures.

Recent legislation such as the *Government Performance and Results Act* and the *Chief Financial Officers Act* has increased the need for you to monitor performance through various performance measures. Performance measures are associated with the outputs of activities. The performance measures for ABC&P focus on how the performance of activities within a process link together as opposed to measuring the performance of the process as a whole. As with cost drivers, selecting appropriate performance measures is more of an art than a science.

Performance measures serve as indicators of how efficiently and effectively an activity is being performed. Efficiency measures monitor the output of an activity in relation to the resources used to produce that output. Cost per unit output is an example of a typical performance measure used to monitor efficiency. Comparing the actual resource usage to a standard resource usage is another common method of measuring efficiency.

Effectiveness measures may be quantitative or qualitative and focus on the following four general areas:

- *Quantity* - measures the number of products produced or the level of service provided by the activity. Examples include inventory fill rates and the number of products provided in a given time period.

Exhibit 3-6   Identifying appropriate drivers is a vital but complex process.

An ABC&P design team at a division of a Fortune 100 electronics company was charged with determining the cost driver for the "Product Engineering" activity. The team identified 15 potential drivers for the activity, and rated each potential driver on the basis of five evaluation criteria. First, potential drivers were scored as having a positive influence, negative influence, or no influence (+1, -1, or 0) on the objective of each evaluation criteria. These values were then multiplied by the relative weightings of the evaluation criteria to arrive at a score. On this basis, "Repair Time" and "Test and Repair Time" tied as the best choice for an activity driver, with "Turn-On Rate" being in second place. The results of this team analysis are presented in the table below:

Potential Driver	Accuracy	Design Influence	Ease of Measuring	Predictability	Availability of Data	Score
Turn-On Rate	+1	0	0	0	-1	9
Repair Time	+1	+1	+1	0	0	18
Cycle Time	0	0	+1	0	0	3
Test & Repair Time	+1	+1	+1	0	0	18
Number of Product Change Orders	-1	-1	+1	-1	+1	-13
Number of Parts	-1	+1	+1	+1	+1	1
Number of Products	-1	-1	+1	0	+1	-11
Number of Specifications	0	0	+1	+1	+1	6
Warranty Rate	0	0	+1	0	+1	4
Material $	0	0	+1	+1	+1	6
Number of Critical Parts	+1	-1	-1	+1	-1	3
Life Cycle	-1	-1	+1	0	0	-12
Manufacturing Overhead $	0	-1	+1	+1	+1	1

KEY

Relative Weight for Each Column	**+** Positive Relationship
	- Negative Relationship
	0 Neutral

- *Quality* - measures how well the output of an activity satisfies established requirements. Examples include the number of products that require rework and the number of errors.

- *Timeliness* - measures how often the activity is completed within the allotted amount of time. Customer wait times and variance between actual cycle time and required cycle time are examples of timeliness measures.

- *Customer Satisfaction* - measures how well the activity output meets the needs and expectations of customers or end users[5]. The number of returns and customer complaints (number and reason for complaint) are examples of performance measures of customer satisfaction[6].

No one measure can be used to measure the effectiveness of the process because performance in all four areas is interrelated. For example, an increase in quantity may adversely affect the quality of the output. It is therefore necessary to monitor effectiveness in all areas jointly to understand the tradeoffs involved and to maximize the effectiveness achieved in all areas.

Define performance measures that are easily measured and interpreted. Focus on aspects of the activities that are under your control, and that help you to identify areas that represent opportunities for improvement. Identify the performance measures for activities that will guide employee actions toward improvement when it is time to design the new business process. Enter the cost drivers and performance measures you identify into the activity database as characteristics of the activity.

COLLECT DATA

Collect data to obtain the values of resource costs, resource drivers, activity drivers, cost drivers, and performance measures. The time period to be studied, sources of data, types of cost data available, and the level of aggregation are all issues to consider in collecting data. As you collect the data, enter it into the activity and product databases that were set up when the activities and products were identified.

Time Period for Data Collection

Determine the period of time for which you want to collect cost and performance measurement data. Base the time period on availability of data and your objectives for ABC&P implementation. Your primary concern in

---

[5] A customer or end user as it is used here refers to the person or process that receives the activity output. In this sense, a customer can be an activity that receives this output as an input.

[6] The specific areas of focus for measuring effectiveness may vary. The areas listed here are consistent with the areas of focus recommended in *Key Criteria for Performance Measurement* distributed by the DoD Comptroller's Office.

CHOOSING PERFORMANCE MEASURES THAT BECOME COST DRIVERS

Telephones arrive by mail or off of a truck at the delivery dock with a letter from the customer attached. This letter lists the telephone's serial number and explains any problems. Then, a repair facility employee completes a Repair Order (RO). As part of the "Forward Telephone with RO to Testing Station" activity, the RO is matched with the telephone and sent to be tested. For this activity, Chris chose the percentage of error in matching ROs with phones as the performance measure. She calculated a 5% error rate.

This performance measure becomes a cost driver for two downstream activities "Test Low Complexity Phones" and "Test High Complexity Phones." While performing these activities, if workers find that a telephone does not have the problem reported in the RO, they check the serial number on the RO and make sure it matches the telephone. If it does not, they send the telephone and RO back to have the correct RO attached and the telephone re-tested. This 5% inaccuracy rate meant that these activities worked on 5% of the telephones twice, which added 5% to their total costs.

choosing a time period is to prevent random or non-indicative variations from distorting reported activity costs and performance measurements. Collect data over a period sufficiently long so that random variations in activities, or variations caused by unusual circumstances not indicative of the activities under consideration, do not skew the results. Determining the appropriate minimum time period requires understanding how activity costs and performance change over time and applying good judgment.

Available Sources

To implement ABC&P cost-effectively, use existing cost and performance data whenever practical. DoD organizations have implemented various accounting systems compliant with the general guidance in DoD 7220.9-M. Additional cost information may be available from budget projections and other sources.

You may also need to "engineer" some costs when you cannot extract them from existing financial systems. For example, an activity might need to account for facility costs, yet the accounting system provides no data for making this calculation. A knowledge of the types of resources used by the modeled activities and the data available from the existing accounting system will help you determine when additional data needs to be collected.

Collecting non-financial performance data offers a similar challenge because it is often not captured at the activity level. As organizations begin to respond to the *Government Performance and Results Act*, this problem should diminish.

Cost Type

Actual costs, budget costs, and standard costs are the three types of costs most often identified in DoD costing systems. Any one of these cost types may be the best to use, depending on the situation.

ABC&P requires that you identify, collect, and trace resource consumption to the responsible activities. This cost data may be found in several forms. In DoD cost systems there are typically three types of costs: actual cost, budgeted cost, and standard cost. These are defined below.

Actual cost is the exact cost paid for a product, including labor, facilities, and other factors of production. Actual costs are current, therefore they reflect existing conditions better than the other types of costs. However, actual costs are also the most variable over time, because they tend to quickly mirror changes in business conditions. Short-term changes are more likely to mask long-term trends when using actual costs.

Budgeted cost is the cost expected to be incurred in some future time period (as documented in DoD's Programming, Planning, and Budgeting System). Budgeted costs can be very useful when tracing costs to activities in As-Is models. However, budgets sometimes represent a wish list of managers' hopes, rather than a realistic assessment of what will most likely result from Congressional appropriations. Use budget information cautiously, particularly in a rapidly changing environment. Budget information may be the only cost data available for costing As-Is models. Using budget data in such cases is a compromise that may be appropriate if actual or standard cost data availability is limited.

Standard cost is the cost that an industrial engineering study says a product "should" cost. These costs are used to determine the resource cost totals to be assigned through activities to products in an ABC&P analysis.

The standard, which may be based either on a theoretically optimum cost or on a practical cost, enables variance analysis by comparing it with actual costs. The disadvantage of standard costing is that it reflects a stagnant view of cost and provides little incentive for continuous improvement.

Your selection of the type of costs to use depends on both the objective of your ABC&P project and the availability of data. Each offers advantages and disadvantages that must also be weighed when making your decision.

Level of Cost Aggregation

Your final consideration in collecting data is the level of needed cost aggregation. Costs are incurred and collected in an accounting system. These costs are aggregated by type and organization, sometimes through several organizational levels, before being reported in a Chart of Accounts. Costs by type and organization may be reported at more than one level of aggregation. For example, military salaries and military benefits may be aggregated to derive military labor costs, and in turn military and civilian labor costs may be aggregated to derive total labor costs.

Activities are performed by organizations or individuals. The hierarchical level of an organization responsible for a particular activity may be well below that reported by the existing accounting system(s). For example, an ABC&P project might be implemented for a procurement activity at a military depot, yet costs for facilities, personnel, utilities, etc. might be reported at the overall depot level. Thus, the accounting system may not report costs at an organizational level low enough to be easily assigned to activities. This problem can be resolved by assigning costs by resource drivers, as described later in this chapter.

ABC&P may also be undertaken at an organizational level higher than where costs are initially recorded. For example, an ABC&P model for the Defense Logistics Agency might require aggregating a depot's costs with other depots' costs to arrive at depot-related activity costs for the Agency. In aggregating costs in this manner, the primary caution is to ensure consistency of data among sources (the depots in this example). For example, are the labor costs reported by the various depots collected in the same manner, and are the same fringe benefits included or excluded from the reported costs?

After you address all data collection issues, you can collect the necessary data through a variety of methods. As discussed in Chapter 2, interviews, questionnaires, workshops, and existing documentation are all good techniques for collecting data.

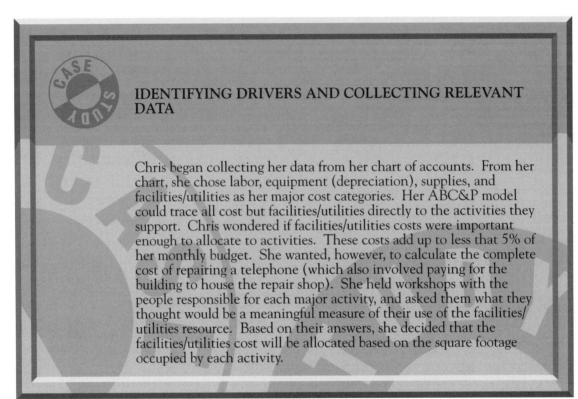

IDENTIFYING DRIVERS AND COLLECTING RELEVANT DATA

Chris began collecting her data from her chart of accounts. From her chart, she chose labor, equipment (depreciation), supplies, and facilities/utilities as her major cost categories. Her ABC&P model could trace all cost but facilities/utilities directly to the activities they support. Chris wondered if facilities/utilities costs were important enough to allocate to activities. These costs add up to less that 5% of her monthly budget. She wanted, however, to calculate the complete cost of repairing a telephone (which also involved paying for the building to house the repair shop). She held workshops with the people responsible for each major activity, and asked them what they thought would be a meaningful measure of their use of the facilities/ utilities resource. Based on their answers, she decided that the facilities/utilities cost will be allocated based on the square footage occupied by each activity.

CALCULATE ACTIVITY COSTS

Cost element: each resource consumed by an activity and its associated cost

Activity cost pool: all cost elements associated with an activity and their total cost

Bill of costs: break-out of the specific cost elements within a cost pool for an activity

The cost of an activity is determined by the cost of the resources it consumes. Each resource consumed by an activity and its associated cost is referred to as a *cost element* of that activity. Cost elements for an activity are grouped together into an *activity cost pool* and the sum of all the cost elements in an activity cost pool provides the total cost of the resources used by that activity. The *bill of costs* provides the break-out of the specific cost elements within a cost pool for an individual activity.

After you identify a resource driver for every cost element within an activity cost pool, assign costs from the appropriate cost system to the various activity cost pools. There are several ways of assigning these resource costs to activities. The accuracy of this assignment varies accord-

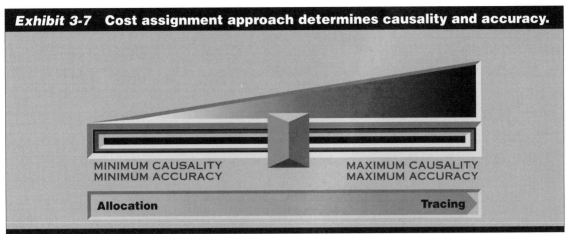

Exhibit 3-7 **Cost assignment approach determines causality and accuracy.**

MINIMUM CAUSALITY
MINIMUM ACCURACY

MAXIMUM CAUSALITY
MAXIMUM ACCURACY

Allocation

Tracing

ing to the degree to which you can establish a causal relationship, as illustrated in **Exhibit 3-7.**

To illustrate the assignment of resource costs, consider the process of training employees. Assume a human resources department of a particular organization is responsible for conducting a mandatory awareness training class for all 25,000 employees of the organization. The department is interested in assigning the cost of its resources to the activities and product of this process. Each class will have 25 participants, requiring 1000 classes to train all employees. A sample bill of cost for one activity (the "Teach Class" activity) in this process is illustrated in **Exhibit 3-8**.

The assignment of labor costs to the "Teach Class" activity in Exhibit 3-8 illustrates the use of tracing. In this case, the resource driver is the number of hours spent teaching the class. The resource driver rate is calculated as follows:

Total number of hours for Human Resources Staff = 50,000
Total labor cost for Human Resources Staff = $ 1,500,000

$$\text{Cost per hour} = \frac{\text{Total labor cost}}{\text{Total \# of hours}} = \frac{\$1,500,000}{50,000} = \$30/\text{ hour}$$

The cost of labor assigned to this activity is calculated by multiplying the number of hours used by this activity by the resource driver rate as calculated above. For this example, the total number of hours necessary for teaching classes is 4000. This figure of 4000 hours is multiplied by $30/hour

Exhibit 3-8 This sample bill of costs illustrates assigning costs to activities.

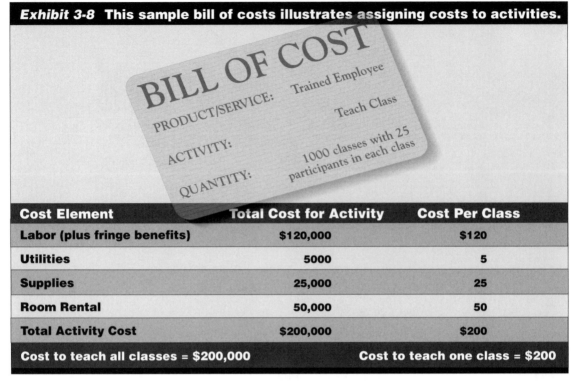

BILL OF COST

PRODUCT/SERVICE: Trained Employee

ACTIVITY: Teach Class

QUANTITY: 1000 classes with 25 participants in each class

Cost Element	Total Cost for Activity	Cost Per Class
Labor (plus fringe benefits)	$120,000	$120
Utilities	5000	5
Supplies	25,000	25
Room Rental	50,000	50
Total Activity Cost	$200,000	$200
Cost to teach all classes = $200,000		Cost to teach one class = $200

to obtain a cost of $120,000 for the labor necessary for the activity of "Teach Class."

In contrast, the assignment of utility costs to the activity "Teach Class" in Exhibit 3-8 illustrates the use of allocation. Because no direct measure of utility usage by this activity exists, the cost of utilities is assigned to the activity "Teach Class" based on a measure of the percentage of time spent by the human resources department on this activity. The cost of utilities is calculated by multiplying the total utility cost by the percentage of time spent on this activity. In this example, if the percentage of time spent teaching classes is eight percent and the total cost of utilities is $62,500, the utility cost assigned to the "Teach Class" activity is .08 x $62,500 or $5000. The costs for the other cost elements for the activity "Teach Class" are calculated in a similar fashion.

In some cases, assigning costs may take more subjective approaches. In such cases direct or substitute measures for tracing and allocating resources to activities (i.e., resource drivers) may not exist or may be impossible to collect in a cost effective way. Also, the historical data for the costs

USING COST ESTIMATING TO ASSIGN COSTS

Chris used cost estimating to assign facility costs to activities. She performed the following steps to estimate the facility costs necessary before assigning them.

1. She estimated the total costs of the facility by determining its replacement cost. (The cost of rebuilding or moving to a comparable facility). This cost is $1 million.

2. She calculated the depreciation on the facility by depreciating the replacement value over the expected life of the facility. Her annual depreciation is $50,000 per year for a $1 million facility with a 20 year expected life.

3. She then calculated the percentage of cost used by each activity. First she measured the total area of the facility (100,000 sq. ft.) and then the area occupied by the people performing each activity. One particular activity takes up 2000 sq. ft., so it is 2% of the total facility. She continued this process for the rest of the activities.

4. She then figured the activity's prorated share of facility depreciation expense by multiplying the total facility cost ($50,000/yr) by the percentage of activity use (2%) to get $1000/yr. She continued this process for the rest of the activities.

themselves may not exist, or the cost of additional collection may not be warranted given the increased level of accuracy that would result. In these situations, you can use interviews and surveys to either trace or allocate resource consumption to activity cost pools. **Exhibit 3-9** illustrates one such subjective approach.

In extreme cases, the accounting system may provide no data, and you will need to use personal insight and judgment to estimate costs in meaningful ways.

CALCULATE PRODUCT COSTS

The total cost of producing a product is that portion of an organization's

Exhibit 3-9 Subjective cost assignment methods are sometimes necessary.

An organization has five cost centers (C1 through C5) that support five activities (A1 through A5). A cost center is an organizational unit at which costs are collected. Assume that all of the centers listed are included in the ABC&P model. One approach for assigning the cost centers to the activities is to ask each cost center to estimate the percentage of a particular resource (personnel, facilities, etc.) it uses in performing or contributing to a particular process. Cost center estimates for the civilian labor used to perform or support each activity are listed in the table below (similar assignments would be done separately for all other cost elements).

Cost Element = Civilian Labor

ACTIVITIES

Cost Center	A1	A2	A3	A4	A5	Totals
C1	10%		60%	30%		100%
C2		83			17	100
C3	34	66				100
C4	50				50	100
C5			80		20	100

Because the percentages support only the listed activities, the total for a given cost center adds up to 100 percent. If this was not the case, only the portion of the resources used by the center would be assigned. In this example, 10 percent of C1's civilian labor supports activity A1, 60 percent supports activity A3, and 30 percent supports activity A4. The percentage of cost center resources used to perform or support a particular process are then multiplied by the total cost for that cost element for that cost center. This provides the cost of a particular resource expended by a specific cost center in support of a specific activity. The total civilian labor costs for each cost center are listed in the far right column in the table below.

Cost Element = Civilian Labor

ACTIVITIES

Cost Center	A1	A2	A3	A4	A5	Totals
C1	$10,000		$60,000	$30,000		$100,000
C2		$24,900			$5,100	$30,000
C3	5,100	9,900				$15,000
C4	2,000				2,000	$4,000
C5			40,000		10,000	$50,000
Total	$17,100	$34,800	$100,000	$30,000	$17,100	$199,000

To calculate the total cost for each activity, this exercise was repeated for the remaining cost elements and the resulting activity costs were added.

resource consumption that can be logically traced or allocated to a particular product. The first step is to distinguish among activity types.

Distinguish Among Primary, Secondary, and Sustaining Activities

Activities can be classified as one of three main types according to the role they play in the organization: primary, secondary, and sustaining. *Primary activities* are those activities that contribute directly to a final product. Because primary activities directly benefit products, you should assign the cost of a primary activity directly to the product that benefits from performing the activity.

Secondary activities play a supporting role to primary activities. You should assign the costs incurred by secondary activities to the primary activities they support. Make this assignment in proportion to the use of the secondary activity by each primary activity. Determine whether or not an activity is primary or secondary based on the purpose of your project and how you define your products. The relationship between primary and secondary activities is illustrated in **Exhibit 3-10.**

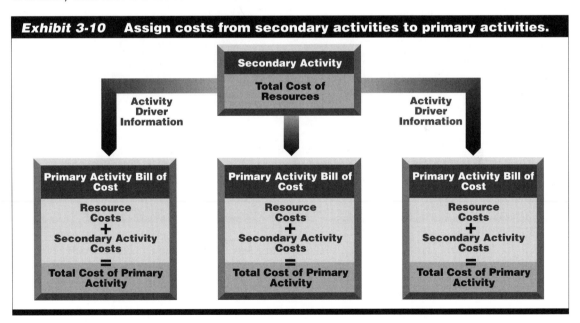

Exhibit 3-10   Assign costs from secondary activities to primary activities.

Sustaining activities support the organization or the process as a whole. They make it possible to do business, but do not directly benefit particular products or primary activities. Typical examples of sustaining activities are the maintenance of the facilities, research and development efforts, and management provided by staff organizations. Because the benefit of the support provided by sustaining activities cannot be attributed to individual products, do not attempt to attribute the costs of sustaining activities to products.

In the context of BPR, sustaining activities are relevant when they have a significant effect on the process being studied and can be controlled. The number of sustaining activities that fall into this category may be small, but understanding the cost of these activities is important as they may be good candidates for reengineering. Determine the cost of these activities and treat them as period expenses. Recognize the cost of the activity and report it, but do not include it in the cost of the product.

Assign Secondary Activity Costs to Primary Activities

After distinguishing among the different types of activities, you need to determine the cost impact of the secondary activities on the primary activities. Assign secondary activities to primary activities through a driver. You can view this driver as an activity driver because it traces the

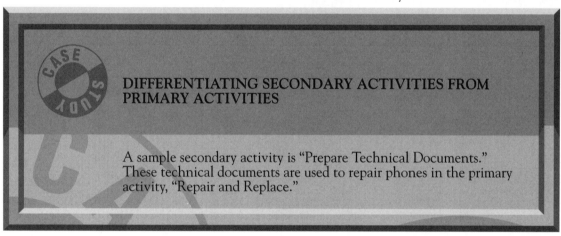

CASE STUDY

DIFFERENTIATING SECONDARY ACTIVITIES FROM PRIMARY ACTIVITIES

A sample secondary activity is "Prepare Technical Documents." These technical documents are used to repair phones in the primary activity, "Repair and Replace."

consumption of the secondary activity to the objective of that activity.

One way to assign secondary activity costs to primary activities is to use interviews and surveys to obtain information regarding the use of the secondary activities by the primary activities. You can interview or survey managers and other key personnel that provide and use secondary activities to get information for describing the relationship among these activities. Based on the information you collect, you can construct a matrix indicating the relationship among primary and secondary activities. **Exhibit 3-11** illustrates the construction of a matrix for assigning secondary activities to primary activities.

Exhibit 3-11 A matrix offers one method for assigning secondary activity costs.

Assume there are three secondary activities S1 through S3 whose costs must be assigned to four primary activities, P1 through P4. On the basis of interviews and surveys with key personnel, analysts estimate the percentage that each secondary activity supports the primary activities.

Secondary Activity Percentage Estimates

	P1	P2	P3	P4	Total (%)
S1	25	25	25	25	100
S2	≈33		≈33	≈33	100
S3		10		90	100

These percentages are then coordinated with key personnel from whom the information was initially gathered to ensure validity. Revisions are made as necessary to best reflect the consensus viewpoint.

After the secondary activities have been apportioned among the supported primary activities, the percentages are multiplied by the cost of each secondary activity to determine the cost to be assigned from each secondary activity to the supported primary activities. This second step is indicated in the table below.

Assignment of Secondary Activity Costs to Primary Activities

	P1	P2	P3	P4	Total $
S1	$15	$15	$15	$15	$60
S2	25		25	25	75
S3		4		36	40
Totals	$40	$19	$40	$76	$175

Assign Primary Activity Costs to Products

Because the cost of secondary activities are assigned to primary activities, you should only assign costs of primary activities to products, as illustrated in **Exhibit 3-12**.

A useful way of viewing these activity costs is through a bill of activities. A bill of activities for a particular product shows the cost of each of the primary activities. To create a bill of activities, calculate the cost per

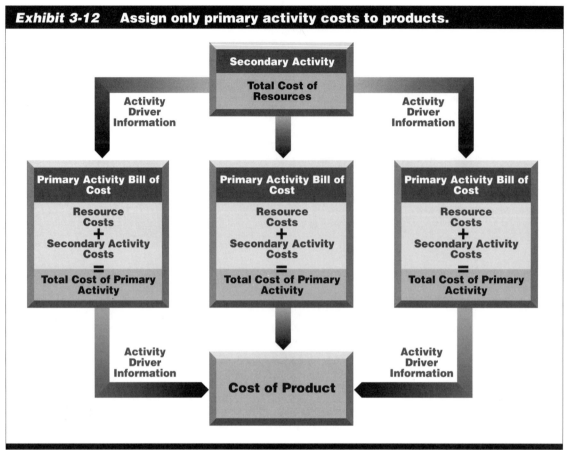

Exhibit 3-12   Assign only primary activity costs to products.

product for each activity used to produce that product. Sum the per product costs for all of these activities to obtain a total product cost. **Exhibit 3-13** is a bill of activities for conducting training, the same example used to illustrate the assignment of resource costs to activities. The trained employee is the product for which a cost was calculated.

Exhibit 3-13 shows the total list of primary activities involved in training employees. Scheduling, conducting follow-up questionnaires, and recording attendance are accomplished separately in this example for every employee. Assume, however, that classes are administered for 25 employees at a time. This means that 1000 classes will be taught to train 25,000 employees. Similarly, one syllabus will be developed and used to teach the classes to all employees.

Activities have been categorized by unit and batch level drivers. Total activity costs for training 25,000 employees are listed under *Total Activity*

Exhibit 3-13 A bill of activities is a useful way to illustrate activity costs.

BILL OF ACTIVITIES

PRODUCT/SERVICE: Trained Employee

QUANTITY: 25,000 Employees

Unit Level Costs	Total Activity Cost	Activity Cost Per Transaction	Activity Cost Per Employee
Schedule Employee	$25,000	$1	$1
Conduct Follow-up	75,000	3	3
Record Attendance	25,000	1	1
Batch Level Costs			
Develop Syllabus (1)	$100,000	$100,000	$4
Teach Class (1000)	200,000	200	8
Total	**$425,000**		**$17**
Cost to train one employee = $17			

Cost in the first column. The activity cost per activity transaction is listed in the second column. For batch level activities, the second column represents the cost of performing one batch. In this example, a batch is either teaching a class to a group of 25 employees, or developing one syllabus for teaching all 25,000 employees. Finally, the activity cost per trained employee and the total cost per trained employee (the product) are listed in the third column.

For unit drivers, there is a direct relationship between the cost per unit and the number of units. More specifically, the activity cost per employee equals the activity cost per transaction times the number of transactions per trained employee. However, for batch drivers, an indirect relationship exists between the cost per unit and the size of the batch. Increasing or decreasing the batch size will decrease or increase the cost per unit respectively.

For the activity "Teach Class," the activity driver is the number of times classes are taught. The activity driver rate is calculated by dividing the total cost of teaching classes by the number of transactions, or the number of classes taught. In Exhibit 3-13, the cost of teaching classes is $200,000 and is divided by 1000 (the number of times classes are taught) to arrive at a cost of $200 to teach one class. The cost per batch is then divided by the batch size to yield the cost per product. In Exhibit 3-13, the batch cost of $200 is divided by the number of employees per batch or 25 employees to arrive at a cost of $8 per employee to teach a class.

Bills of cost and bills of activities are useful management tools for better understanding the sources of cost, and for helping steer BPR initiatives.

TRADITIONAL COSTING VERSES ABC&P

After completing the ABC&P model, Chris calculated the costs to see how these differed from the cost data provided by the traditional accounting system. She built the following chart:

	ABC&P	Accounting System
One Low Complexity Unit, Walk-In	$22.15	$15.09
One Low Complexity Unit, Mail lot 50	13.56	15.09
One High Complexity Unit, Walk-In	26.03	21.21
One High Complexity Unit, Mail lot 50	$17.44	$21.21

ABC&P calculated the cost of fixing the same telephones as being higher in some cases and lower in others when compared to the same costs calculated with traditional accounting techniques. For example, a low complexity telephone from a walk-in costs $7 more to repair when costed with ABC&P than with traditional costing methods. Chris realized from this more accurate figure that she needed to evaluate the process of fixing this type of telephone more closely. After evaluating this process, Chris knew she would be able to act on one (or a combination) of the following three options: drop the service, charge more for it, or reduce costs incurred in performing this activity.

The bill of activities also shows, in quantifiable terms, the costs you will save by eliminating a particular activity.

SUMMARY

Establishing the As-Is Baseline involves five major steps:

- Develop the As-Is activity model
- Identify all ABC&P components
- Collect data
- Calculate activity costs
- Calculate product costs

The "Develop the As-Is Activity Model" step involves developing a graphic representation of the activities that compose the business process you are studying. The "Identify all ABC&P Components" step involves defining the products and activities you wish to cost, and identifying the associated resources, resource drivers, activity drivers, cost drivers, and performance measures. The "Collect Data" step entails addressing data issues (e.g. the time period for data collection, the type of data to use, the availability of data) and then using a variety of data collection techniques to collect data pertaining to resource costs, resource drivers, activity drivers, cost drivers, and performance measures. Use resource driver information to then determine activity costs in the "Calculate Activity Costs" step. The final step is "Calculate Product Costs." It involves using activity costs and activity driver information to determine product costs. You can then use your ABC&P baseline to analyze and compare the cost and performance of a process and identify opportunities for improvement.

CHAPTER 1
CHAPTER 2
CHAPTER 3
CHAPTER 4

ABC
Performance

Using ABC&P
Results to Design
New Business
Practices

I like the dreams of the future better than the history of the past.

– THOMAS JEFFERSON

CHAPTER 4: USING ABC&P RESULTS TO DESIGN NEW BUSINESS PRACTICES

A BC&P provides you with insights into costs and performance that highlight the potential for improvements in your processes. You can apply these insights to your As-Is model in your BPR effort to achieve significant cost savings and increased performance. This chapter describes the role of ABC&P in designing new business practices, and tools and analysis techniques to use to get the most from ABC&P during the course of your BPR project. The chapter is organized into the following sections:

- Focus the improvement effort on high impact activities
- Analyze improvement opportunities
- Develop and analyze To-Be models

FOCUS THE IMPROVEMENT EFFORT ON HIGH IMPACT ACTIVITIES

Recognizing that you may not be able to improve all activities within a process at once, it is important you focus your efforts on the high cost activities and high payoff improvement opportunities. Your goal is to maximize return on improvement investments. For example, achieving a

Maximize your return on investment by focusing your improvement effort on activities with the highest payoff potential.

25 percent cost reduction in an activity that accounts for 60 percent of overall process costs is much more beneficial than achieving the same cost reduction for an activity that accounts for only 15 percent of overall process costs. The most practical approach may be to first perform a high level analysis of activities to determine high cost activities and high payoff opportunities, and then perform detailed modeling and analysis selectively.

Two tools you can use to evaluate ABC&P results and focus on high impact activities are Pareto analysis and interrelationship diagraphs.

Pareto Analysis

Pareto Analysis is a method for identifying high cost activities. It is based on the "80/20 rule" that assumes that 20 percent of what you do accounts for 80 percent of your business. In the context of a BPR project, assume that 20 percent of your activities generally account for 80 percent of your costs.

Pareto analysis involves ranking the activity costs you calculated as part of your ABC&P analysis in decreasing order to highlight the high cost activities. Choose one activity level and include all the activities within that level in the analysis. Choose a level that provides sufficient detail to illustrate distinctions among the activity costs. Next, develop a bar chart showing the total cost devoted to each activity. Arrange the bars in the chart in descending order from left to right. This allows you to quickly identify the activities that cost the most. Focus improvement and cost reduction efforts on the activities that account for the majority of costs.

Interrelationship Diagraphs

Another way to maximize your return on investments for your improvements is to focus improvement efforts on the activities that have the greatest impact on other activities. Interrelationship diagraphing[1] helps identify all of the logical relationships among activities within a process. Understanding these relationships provides useful insights into how improvements made to one activity affect other activities. There are several methods for developing interrelationship diagraphs. **Exhibit 4-1** outlines the steps for one of these methods.

---

[1] Brassard, Michael. *The Memory Jogger Plus™*, (Goal/QPC, Methuen, MA), 1989, pp. 41-71.

Exhibit 4-1 One method for Interrationship Diagraphs uses yellow post-it notes.

Identify the activities to include in your interrelationship diagraph. Choose activities from your As-Is ABC&P model that have a sufficient amount of detail to distinguish them from other activities. Make sure that these activities all have the same level of detail; they will most likely be high level activities. Write the name of each activity on a separate yellow post-it note. You will place these post-it notes one by one on a white board to create your interrelationship diagraph.

Pick an activity from the group* and ask what other activity is caused by or results from this activity. Place the first 2 activities on a white board or paper easle and draw an arrow from the causing activity to the effected activity to illustrate the relationship between the activities. In many cases, the relationship can go both ways. Pick the cause and effect direction that is most influential.

Once you complete this process, have all team members and stakeholders review the resulting interrelationship diagraph. Revise it as necessary to make it accurate.

Repeat the process described in step 3 until all activities have been added to the board. Keep in mind as you add activities that you are not looking for primary relationships, but all relationships among the activities. In determining relationships, allow for some discussion, but do not get bogged down by details.

One by one, pick activities and place them on the board, drawing the appropriate relationships with arrows. Once again, choose the more influential relationship when both exist. Use performance measures and cost drivers to help identify relationships; activities that share common performance measures and cost drivers are generally related.

* Selecting the activities in random order encourages people to think of the relationships among activities in a way other than in the usual order in which the activities are performed. This enables people to recognize the relationships that may have been missed before.

Note: The steps outlined above work best for a group of fifteen or fewer activities. If more than fifteen activities are to be included, you may want to develop a matrix for the exercise, instead of using post-it notes and a white board. To do this, list all activities on both axes. Follow the same basic process of determining the relationships among activities, but draw the appropriate arrows on the matrix at the intersection of the two activities.

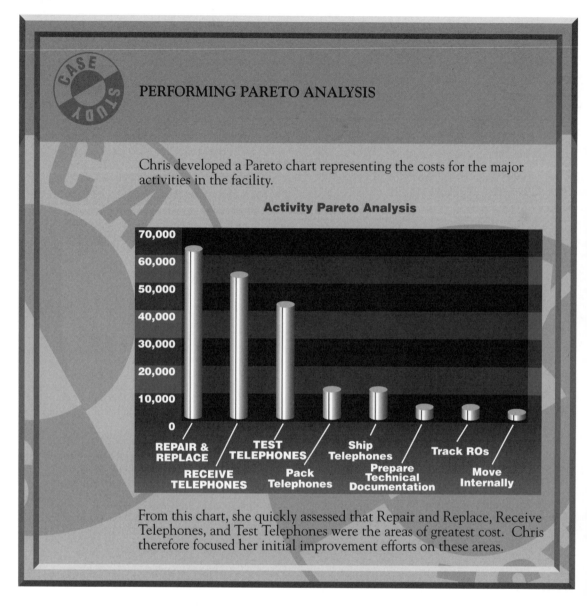

PERFORMING PARETO ANALYSIS

Chris developed a Pareto chart representing the costs for the major activities in the facility.

Activity Pareto Analysis

From this chart, she quickly assessed that Repair and Replace, Receive Telephones, and Test Telephones were the areas of greatest cost. Chris therefore focused her initial improvement efforts on these areas.

After creating an interrelationship diagraph, identify the activities that have the most arrows exiting them. A large number of arrows exiting an activity indicates the activity impacts many other activities. Improving this activity will likely have a positive result on the activities it impacts. A large number of arrows entering a particular activity warns of a potential bottleneck in the process. These activities are also good candidates for improvement.

Evaluate the results of the interrelationship diagraph to decide the final list of activities on which to focus your improvement efforts. The scope, budget, time, and other constraints associated with your BPR project will influence how many of these activities you can analyze.

ANALYZE IMPROVEMENT OPPORTUNITIES

After you target high cost and high impact activities to reengineer, you must identify specific ways in which you can improve these activities. This is often the most challenging step in a BPR effort because it requires imagination and vision. Successful BPR projects are based on a thorough understanding of the current environment and how changes will affect the environment. Applying technology, changing the organizational structure, reordering the way things are done, and making other changes to business processes all impact the environment. ABC&P helps you understand these impacts. Tools that can help you analyze improvement opportunities include paradigm analysis, value-added analysis, benchmarking, and best practices analysis.

Paradigm Analysis

"A paradigm is a set of rules (written or unwritten) that does two things: (1) it establishes or defines boundaries; and (2) it tells how to behave inside the boundaries in order to be successful."[2] Whether your BPR effort involves radically changing the way you perform business or merely streamlining current practices, it will require change. Change is difficult because it challenges paradigms. Developing an acceptance of and willingness to change is essential to the success of any BPR effort. Paradigm analysis helps you understand and eliminate the constraints of current practices so you can identify and institute improved ways to perform activities.

Paradigm: a set of rules (written or unwritten) that establishes or defines boundaries and tells how to behave inside the boundaries to be successful.

A paradigm creates expectations and serves as an information filter. People tend to accept information that agrees with the expectations established by the paradigm, while ignoring or distorting information that conflicts with the paradigm. This can sometimes be beneficial in problem solving because it helps people focus their attention on the important

---

[2] Barker, Joel. *Future Edge*. (William Morrow and Company, Inc., New York, NY), 1992, p. 32.

information. However, paradigms can also have negative effects, especially when the paradigm restricts people to only one way of thinking. This can prevent people from recognizing opportunities, adopting improved business practices, or discovering new solutions to problems. Paradigms may also provide a false sense of security. People may reject changes, even those that are clearly beneficial, because they are blinded by their investments and past successes in their current paradigms.

Different paradigms often generate different solutions to the same problem. In fact, the solution to a problem may be difficult for people in one paradigm to see, but be obvious to people outside of that paradigm. Outsiders are often responsible for significant innovations because they are not restricted by the rules of existing paradigms.[3] An excellent example of an innovation made possible by challenging existing paradigms is the invention of the airplane. The Wright brothers challenged the experts' paradigm that heavier than air flight was impossible.

Breaking through the barriers of a paradigm involves continually questioning current business practices and exploring the boundaries of what is possible. Paradigm analysis is usually performed at a high level. The higher the level of analysis, the greater the number of opportunities for change, and in turn, the greater the possibility of real breakthrough and innovation. **Exhibit 4-2** illustrates the analogy of thinking outside the box, a necessary step in breaking through existing paradigms.

The first step of paradigm analysis is challenging the current state by asking the question "why?" about each activity you perform. Ask yourself, "Why do we perform this activity? Why do we perform it in the current manner? Do we perform some activities simply because that is the way it has been done for years? Do we perform activities to meet regulations which no longer exist? Why does it cost so much to perform this activity? Why does it take so long to perform this activity?" Only by questioning current business practices and performance will you develop an awareness of the boundaries of the current paradigm.

Once you understand the current capabilities of the process, challenge these capabilities. Set currently unachievable performance targets and find

---

[3] Barker, Joel. *Future Edge*. (William Morrow and Company, Inc., New York, NY), 1992.

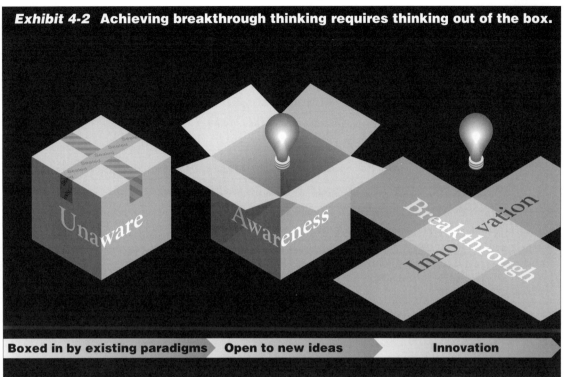

Exhibit 4-2 **Achieving breakthrough thinking requires thinking out of the box.**

Unaware   **Awareness**   **Breakthrough**   **Innovation**

Boxed in by existing paradigms ⟩   **Open to new ideas**   ⟩   **Innovation** ⟩

ways to achieve these targets by asking questions that force you to think beyond the current boundaries. Ask yourself, "Why not? Why can't we perform the activity this way? Why can't we produce this output in less time or with fewer resources? What if this activity were eliminated by part of another activity? How else can we do this activity to obtain the same output, but consume fewer resources?" These questions help you to think outside the box and achieve breakthrough innovation.

Value-Added Analysis

Before improving activities, it is necessary to understand the basic characteristics of the activities, such as why they are performed and what contribution they make to the result of the process. Value-added analysis is a tool for defining the purpose and contribution of activities, evaluating the value they add, and guiding the improvement efforts for each type of activity.

Defining activities as value-added, non-value-added, or non-value-added but required helps focus improvement efforts.

When performing value-added analysis, start by defining the purpose and contribution of the activity and determining the value added by its contribution. In other words, assess if an activity is value-added (contributes to satisfying customer requirements), non-value-added (does not contribute to satisfying customer requirements), or non-value-added but required by regulation, directive, or instruction. While there are several approaches recommended and used for this first phase, it is important to realize that it is the thought process involved that helps you gain the necessary information about the activities, not the specific approach you use. **Exhibit 4-3** outlines a series of key steps for performing this assessment.

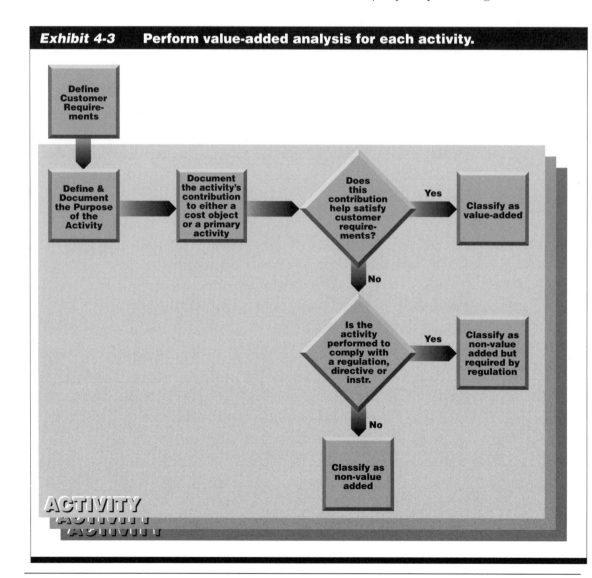

Exhibit 4-3   Perform value-added analysis for each activity.

Determining the purpose and contribution of each activity helps you identify possible problem areas in a current process. If it is difficult to define the purpose of an activity or the contribution made by an activity, it may be unnecessary to perform it. As you encounter these issues, note them and ensure that they are addressed by the new business practices.

Value-added Activities

Understanding the value added by an activity provides you with insights into the goals of the improvement effort for each type of activity. For value-added activities, your goal is to improve how the necessary purposes are accomplished and contribute to the products.

Value-added activities are often the best candidates for reengineering.

Because an activity is classified as value-added does not mean its performance cannot be improved. Improvements to value-added activities have the potential to have the greatest impact on the overall process because they perform the essential functions within the process. While you may change the design of these activities, their purposes must still be accomplished. Focus improvement efforts on finding better, more efficient, and more effective ways to accomplish these purposes.

Begin by evaluating the effectiveness and efficiency of the activity or set of activities you are improving. To evaluate the effectiveness, assess how well the activities' performance satisfies their purposes. Use the performance measures you defined in your ABC&P model to help evaluate effectiveness. These performance measures illustrate how well an activity serves the needs of other activities and/or customers. Redesign activities so that their performance is in line with their intended purpose. When redesigning an activity, it may be beneficial to break it down further to identify the portions of the activity that do not serve the intended purpose. Restructure or eliminate these individual portions based on their usefulness.

To evaluate the activities' efficiency, assess the amount of resources consumed by them. Do these activities consume a reasonable amount of resources in accomplishing their purposes? Use the performance measures and activity costs supplied by your ABC&P analysis; they serve as good indicators of efficiency. The resource drivers, cost drivers, and activity drivers defined in the ABC&P model provide insights into what drives resource consumption. These insights are also useful for redesigning activities to be more efficient.

You can make activities more effective and efficient by combining two or more activities. Determine whether or not the purpose of an inefficient or ineffective activity can be accomplished by another existing activity. This may involve evaluating whether or not an activity is performed simply because another activity is not performed correctly or effectively. Performance measures and cost drivers are useful for this because they identify the reason an activity is performed and how well its performance satisfies the requirements of other activities or external customers. If the activity's performance is poor, combine this activity with other activities, or create one activity that meets the purposes of the original activities in a more efficient and effective manner.

Another way to improve effectiveness and efficiency is to find a better way of accomplishing the activity's purpose. ABC&P analysis provides information about the resources consumed by an activity and the factors that cause this consumption.

You should use this information to evaluate if there are different resources that can be used or different ways to perform the activity to reduce the resource consumption or the cost of the resources consumed. For example, does technology exist that would accomplish the same purpose differently and consume fewer resources? If so, change the method of performing this activity to incorporate the better way of accomplishing the same purpose.

Non-Value-Added Activities

The classification "non-value-added" refers to the value of an activity from the customer's perspective.

Non-value-added activities do not add value to the product from a customer's perspective. This term is often inappropriately interpreted to mean there is no valid reason for the activity to occur. Classifying alternatives as non-value-added is important because it helps focus improvement efforts on external customers. It is also important, however, to recognize that some non-value-added activities may be important to internal customers and other stakeholders. Non-value-added activities can be categorized into four groupings:

- Not required
- Required by the As-Is model
- Required by your organization's mission, objectives, or strategies
- Required by regulation, directive, or instruction

Non-value-added activities that can be classified as "not required" are those that do not serve a purpose. These activities often served a useful purpose at some point in time, but under current conditions are no longer needed. An example is the generation of a report that no longer provides useful information. Recipients of the report probably ignore it, but do not think to tell the person generating the report that it is no longer needed. Removing such non-value-added activities is typically simple. The challenge lies in identifying "not required" activities for what they are. For this reason, challenge every activity's reason for existence. There should always be someone or something (e.g., an information system) ready to claim a need for the output of an activity. If you cannot find such a person or thing with a need for an activity, chances are excellent that the activity is no longer required.

The second group of non-value-added activities are those required by other activities in the As-Is activity model, but that can be eliminated or reduced through BPR. Such activities are not inherently required by the business itself, but rather by *how* the business is currently done. Moving a component from an inventory stock room at one end of a factory to an assembly point at the other end of the factory is an example of such an activity. The movement of the component is essential in getting the part from the stock room to the assembly line as the process is currently performed. However, it may be possible to greatly reduce the cost and time associated with moving the part. Actions such as moving the stock room and assembly points closer together, or moving the components in batches, could help reduce the activity cost.

The third group of non-value-added activities are those required by or supporting the overall mission, objectives, or strategies of the organization. This group is often the source of confusion by individuals that assume "non-value-added" always infers "not required." Activities like marketing or research and development might be labeled as non-value-added from the perspective of the external customer, yet may be important to the organization. In fact, you might need to add resources to some of these activities.

Do not treat labels such as non-value-added as an opportunity to suspend the use of good analysis and judgment. Study the impacts of reductions in resources provided to these activities. Seek ways to improve the efficiency and effectiveness of non-value-added activities that support organizational missions, objectives, or strategies.

An interrelationship diagraph is useful for assessing the impacts of eliminating these activities on other activities. If it is feasible to eliminate the activity, do so. Then, redeploy or eliminate the associated resources. If you cannot eliminate it, ensure that the activity is performed as efficiently and effectively as practical. To do so, use the same procedures as you would for value-added activities.

Some non value-added activities are required by regulation, directive, or instruction. Separate the cost of the regulations associated with a process from the other process costs. If these costs are significant, try to eliminate or improve the activity. Recent efforts to improve the Federal government, such as the National Performance Review, support efforts to eliminate unnecessary regulations, or "red tape." Knowing how much the regulatory aspect of a process costs can help you make a case for eliminating regulations thereby eliminating or improving a non-value added activity.

If you cannot eliminate a regulation that is causing non-value-added activities to be performed, evaluate whether or not the regulation can be simplified. If it can, simplify the activity that supports the regulation and reduce the resources the activity consumes. When it is not possible to eliminate or simplify the regulation, focus on improving the activity alone. If possible, incorporate the compliance functions of the activity into another activity.

If compliance with the regulation requires a separate activity, evaluate the effectiveness and efficiency of the activity and improve it as much as practical. Consider the original intent of the regulation and determine whether it is the actual regulation or simply the interpretation of the regulation that is constraining the process. Then, follow the same steps for improving the activity as for value-added activities.

Benchmarking

Benchmarking is an analytical tool for identifying areas of low performance, prioritizing areas for improvement, and helping define realistic improvement goals. Unlike the analytical tools discussed up to this point, benchmarking helps identify the amount of improvement possible. Benchmarking involves measuring the performance of activities against the performance of similar activities in internal and external organizations considered to be the "best of the best." Do not confuse benchmarking with best practices analysis. You will use the results from benchmarking for best practices analysis, as discussed later in this chapter.

By using external sources to establish improvement targets, you can more easily identify achievable performance levels and you become aware of the changing environment and how it affects performance standards. You can be sure the goals you get from benchmarking are credible, objective, and achievable because another organization has already attained them.

Before beginning your benchmarking effort, develop a clear purpose that is closely tied with the purpose and objectives of your BPR. This is necessary to ensure the results you obtain from benchmarking are usable for improving processes. Remember that the objective of benchmarking is not to criticize past performance, but to understand the areas that need improvement and the magnitude of improvement that is possible. All of the people involved in the effort must have a clear understanding of the purpose of your benchmarking effort or they may become defensive and spend their time and effort justifying their performance instead of generating ideas for improvement. After addressing these preliminary issues, begin benchmarking. The main steps for benchmarking are described in **Exhibit 4-4.**

After gathering benchmarking data, analyze it and transform it into information that is useful for improving performance. You may need to make adjustments to raw data to account for differences between your organization and those you are benchmarking (such as different management strategies, production volumes, and customer requirements). Report your results in an organized manner by using charts or matrices that contain the values of activity metrics for your organization and the organizations you benchmarked. Add these results to your activity database. Verify the findings with the parties involved in the activities being analyzed.

Use the information you gathered from the benchmarking effort to identify areas of low performance, and prioritize improvement efforts

Exhibit 4-4   Benchmarking is a tool for setting realistic goals.

1

Determine the activities to benchmark. Good benchmarking candidates include:

- Activities with the potential to provide significant performance improvements
- High cost activities
- High impact activities
- Value-added activities

2

Determine the benchmarking metrics to use. Metrics are the characteristics of activities compared across organizations. Choose metrics from the characteristics of the resource drivers, activity drivers, cost drivers, and performance measures defined in your ABC&P model. These provide insights into the key factors that drive the costs of activities and are indicators of activity performance.

3

Determine the organizations to benchmark. Identify high performing organizations. Choose the organizations from the following:

- Other functional units within the organization
- Organizations within the same industry
- Leaders of other industries

Good benchmarking candidates include organizations and companies that exhibit good bottom-line performance in terms of profit growth and market share; companies with excellent reputations for quality, customer service, and innovation; and recipients of public recognition awards.

4

Gather data. Gather data regarding how activities are performed, and assign values to the metrics for both your organization and the benchmarking candidate. Note any differences between your organization and the other organizations in terms of size, products, markets, and how they perform activities. Make any necessary adjustments to ensure a meaningful comparison. Existing information (e.g. magazine articles, trade journals, on-line data bases, annual reports, etc.) and original research (interviews, site visits) are two main sources for this data. After gathering data, document it, summarize it, and review it to determine what additional information is necessary and possible sources for gathering this information.

according to the areas found to have the weakest performance. To do this, identify the highest metric value for each performance measurement and calculate the gap between your performance and the best possible performance. Also include this information in the benchmarking chart or matrix. Set quantifiable improvement targets based on the information gained about the level of performance that is possible.

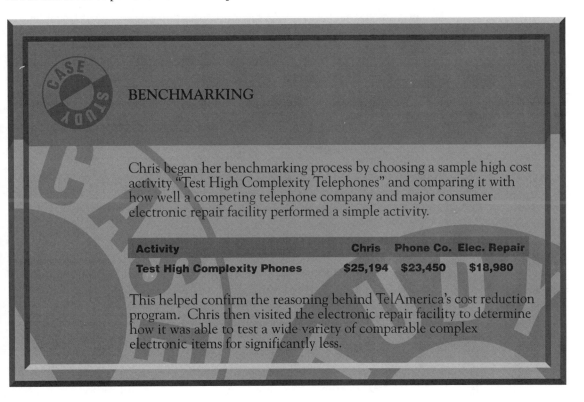

BENCHMARKING

Chris began her benchmarking process by choosing a sample high cost activity "Test High Complexity Telephones" and comparing it with how well a competing telephone company and major consumer electronic repair facility performed a simple activity.

Activity	Chris	Phone Co.	Elec. Repair
Test High Complexity Phones	$25,194	$23,450	$18,980

This helped confirm the reasoning behind TelAmerica's cost reduction program. Chris then visited the electronic repair facility to determine how it was able to test a wide variety of comparable complex electronic items for significantly less.

Best Practices Analysis

Best practices analysis involves learning how industry leaders perform activities that have similar purposes to your activities to help you achieve superior performance. Practices refer to the methods an organization uses to perform business processes. They are the conceptual approaches used to accomplish specific purposes. Best practices analysis helps generate alternative ways of accomplishing similar purposes. You can then analyze the alternative methods to determine how you might be able to incorporate them into the processes you want to improve to help you reach the targets set in your benchmarking effort.

Practices: the methods an organization uses to perform business processes.

To start a best practices analysis, determine the topics or areas of a process that you want to analyze. Choose the candidates for best practices from the ones you used in your benchmarking effort. Perform best practices analysis at a high level where you can group several activities together. Include activities identified as high cost, high impact, low performance, and value-added. Also, choose a variety of organizations for studying best practices so that you can identify both common and unique approaches for performing the activity.

Compare the factors that drive the costs of activities and products in different organizations using ABC&P. Redesign activities so that the factors that cause resource consumption (i.e., the drivers) are consistent with the purpose of the activity. Use the information gathered about drivers at other organizations to restructure your activities so that the factors that drive costs are aligned with the purpose of the activity.

The final step of a best practices analysis is choosing the best alternatives and determining how to adapt them to your process. Make changes that help you attain the improvement goals you set in your benchmarking effort.

DEVELOP AND ANALYZE TO-BE MODELS

The ideas for improvement generated by the analysis performed thus far are used to develop new business practice alternatives. The *CIM Functional Economic Analysis Guidebook* defines an alternative as "a slate of initiatives that can achieve a functional activity's intended To-Be state." As the name and definition imply, an alternative is one of several mutually exclusive ways to perform the process being reengineered. Develop To-Be activity (IDEF0) models for new business practice alternatives to help you select the best alternative.

The previous chapter discussed the characteristics of effective activity models. In designing To-Be models, incorporate these characteristics to enhance the value of the models as tools for understanding how your new practices will fit into your business.

Modeling To-Be processes is key to your BPR effort. The BPR component focuses on the way processes will be performed, stakeholder analysis, customer satisfaction, and product impact. The ABC&P component focuses on the cost and performance aspects of the reengineered processes and the resulting product.

Developing To-Be Models

The steps in developing To-Be activity models are different than those for developing As-Is Models. First, isolate the activities you are reengineering and evaluate their relationships to other activities in the process model. This exercise will help you determine the effort required to build To-Be activity models. At this point, group activities into three categories for each To-Be alternative:

1. Unchanged activities that are not impacted by reengineered activities
2. Unchanged activities that are impacted by reengineered activities
3. Activities that have been added or changed as a result of reengineering

Take the activity model characteristics for the first category of activities directly from the As-Is model and treat them like building blocks for To-Be alternatives. The second and third categories require additional analysis in creating the To-Be model.

At this stage of the reengineering effort, your To-Be models are conceptual in nature. Use them only to provide comparisons for choosing the alternatives deserving additional study. One method for developing potential alternatives is brainstorming, as illustrated in **Exhibit 4-5.**

Examining the alternatives more closely may reveal some alternatives as clearly inferior. They may be impractical, fail to incorporate critical or mandatory actions, or be unresponsive to customer needs. Eliminate these inferior candidates from further consideration. You do not need to use formal analysis to prove a candidate is inferior. Removing an inferior alternative from further consideration only requires confidence that there is no chance of it being the best alternative. This first informal screening is illustrated in **Exhibit 4-6.**

For models that continue to show potential, use ABC&P analysis to further eliminate alternatives from consideration. ABC&P allows you to discriminate between the behavior of cost and performance in the To-Be processes and the As-Is process. Your analysis need only be as precise as minimally necessary to discriminate among alternatives. Refine the To-Be model as you narrow alternatives, as shown in **Exhibit 4-7.**

Exhibit 4-5   Brainstorming is a method for developing alternatives.

Dynamic Simulation in Model Analysis

Dynamic simulation is a useful tool for analyzing an As-Is model or building a To-Be model. Simulation can identify easy-access, high leverage improvement opportunities in the current system. It can also help design the To-Be model by testing various "what-if" scenarios and setting achievable performance expectations.

Understanding Simulation

Simulation is an automated technique that imitates the operation of real-world activities. A simulation model is an abstract representation of a system based on a set of assumptions, and is expressed as mathematical or logical relations between objects. The word *dynamic* introduces the dimension of time into the model, and makes dynamic simulation a valuable tool in BPR efforts.

Exhibit 4-6   **Eliminate obviously inferior alternatives.**

Simulation as a Tool for Analyzing the As-Is Model

The activity model discussed in Chapter 3 is a static snapshot of an enterprise. Unfortunately, when attempting to improve global performance, static models do not tell the whole story. Dynamics must be injected into the model, and the system's behavior must be analyzed over a period of time to understand activity interrelationships and patterns of change.

Simulation provides the ability to study a system's dynamic complexity. It allows you to make improvements to different activities, view performance over time, and analyze the effect on an entire system without ever implementing real changes. Results from this type of analysis tell what or where changes need to be made, but not *how* to make those changes.

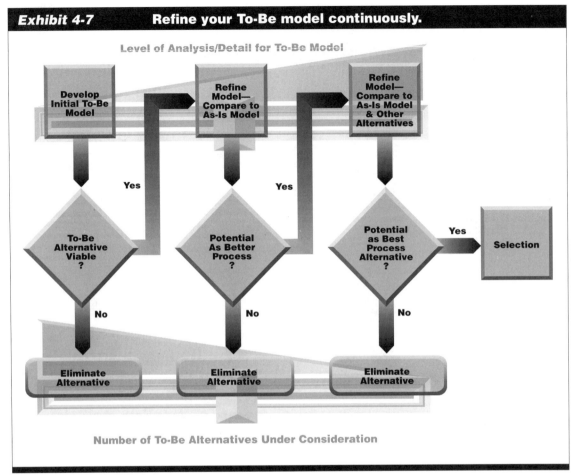

Exhibit 4-7 — **Refine your To-Be model continuously.**

Simulation as a Tool for Designing Your To-Be Model

Designing your To-Be model is not an easy task. When it is time to implement the model, often numerous questions are left unanswered. You can use dynamic simulation to analyze and test sub-systems of your To-Be model and answer many of these questions. Examples of questions include the following:

- How much staffing is needed at this point?
- What level of inventory will satisfy expected demand next year? Three years from now?
- What customer response time is needed?

Simulation helps you perform a "what-if" analysis of different environments, demand scenarios, staff sizes, etc. This technique allows you to rigorously define the new To-Be activity model, take long-term and contingency plans into consideration, and set realistic performance expectations and goals. When using simulation for your analysis, avoid over-modeling. A high level model of the entire process with detailed models for specific pieces is all that is necessary to analyze the To-Be models.

SUMMARY

ABC&P helps you analyze process alternatives, develop To-Be models for these alternatives, understand the differences between the As-Is process and To-Be alternatives, and narrow the alternatives under consideration. At this point in the BPR process, it is important to avoid "over-modeling" To-Be alternatives. The objective is to illustrate differences that serve as discriminators for either eliminating the alternative or taking it forward for decision making. There are several tools that are useful at this stage of the analysis, as summarized in **Exhibit 4-8.**

Exhibit 4-8	Combine analysis tools to design To-Be models.	
Analysis Tool	**ABC&P Insights Used**	**How Tool Supports BPR Effort**
Benchmarking	• factors that drive costs • financial and non-financial performance information	• determines areas of low performance • sets improvement goals
Best Practices Analysis	• factors that drive costs • activities currently performed	• provides a better understanding of how your business performs in comparison to industry leaders • enables you to evaluate (through comparison with the "best of breed") if the focus of your activities is consistent with the purpose of performing them
Dynamic Simulation	• financial and non-financial performance information • activity models	• provides a mechanism for evaluating activity behavior over time providing additional insights into problem areas • allows you to set realistic performance expectations and goals
Interrelationship Diagraphing	• factors that drive costs and performance	• identifies opportunities for high-impact changes
Paradigm Analysis	• factors that drive cost • financial and non-financial performance information • activity models	• provides a better understanding of your current practices and related performance forming the foundation for questioning the current constraints of your process • helps you view your process with the objectivity of an outsider, thereby helping generate new and innovative ideas for improvement
Pareto Analysis	• cost of activities	• identifies high-cost activities by ranking activities in decreasing order of cost
Value-Added Analysis	• financial and non-financial performance information • factors that drive costs	• develops understanding of why activities are performed and the value added by the activity's contribution to the product • helps evaluate effectiveness and efficiency of activities

Using ABC&P
to Select
Alternatives

Alice said, "Would you please tell me which way to go from here?" The cat said, "That depends on where you want to get to."

– LEWIS CARROLL

CHAPTER 5: USING ABC&P TO SELECT ALTERNATIVES

After completing the "design new business practices" stage of your BPR effort, you will have narrowed your broad list of alternatives to a smaller set of viable alternatives from which to select your new business practices. At this point you need to analyze the costs and benefits of each alternative. A formal Cost Benefit Analysis (CBA) will help you estimate, compare, and evaluate the costs and benefits of each alternative and make your final selection. This chapter discusses the steps in performing a CBA and the role ABC&P plays in each step:

- Prepare for your CBA
- Estimate costs and benefits for each alternative
- Compare costs and benefits of alternatives to the As-Is
- Select the best alternative

PREPARE FOR YOUR CBA

Before beginning a CBA, it is important to understand the objectives of the CBA within your BPR project, the role ABC&P will play, and the level of analysis required.

CBA Objectives

A CBA analyzes the financial impacts of alternatives.

The objective of a CBA is not to perfectly assess the alternatives' costs and benefits. In the context of a BPR effort, a CBA has two objectives: to help identify the most cost-effective approach to meeting your BPR objectives, and to evaluate whether your alternatives provide an adequate return on investment. A CBA helps you analyze the financial impacts of alternatives. It does this by condensing large amounts of financial data into an easy-to-understand summary for each alternative in a manner that highlights the economic differences between them and their impacts on the As-Is.

Investing wisely is particularly important in today's environment of constrained budgets. Money for investments is scarce. You must demonstrate that any proposed investment will yield benefits that exceed the cost of implementation by some pre-defined or target amount when compared to the As-Is model.

Augment your CBA with good judgment.

A CBA is not designed to replace judgment. Good decision makers consider more than financial analysis results alone. Selecting your final alternative will involve balancing cost while considering schedule, performance, risk, or other factors important to your particular project. A CBA alone may not capture all of these considerations.

The Role of ABC&P in CBA

A CBA analyzes two types of costs: investment costs and activity costs. Investment costs are the costs required to implement the proposed changes in the business processes. Estimating these costs is relatively straightforward. Activity costs are the operational costs of activities within a process. Activity costs must be estimated for the As-Is as well as the To-Be models being evaluated. Estimating activity costs can be difficult because most organizations do not collect costs by activities, but rather by accounting codes or similar methods. ABC&P helps you to estimate activity costs because it assigns resource costs to activities. By improving the starting point of the CBA, all subsequent analyses become more accurate. The modeling and performance aspects of ABC&P further improve your CBA by forcing you to consider how changes to one activity impact the other activities in a process, ensuring you consider these impacts in your analysis.

Level of Analysis Required

Performing a detailed CBA of every reengineered alternative, even if all are within the project's scope, can rapidly consume your valuable resources. Remember not to spend more resources performing analysis than the value you expect to gain from the resulting information. Concentrate on areas that have the greatest savings potential. Include all costs and benefits relevant to your decision, but do not include costs that are equal or close enough so as to not be discriminators in the selection process. A simple way to save resources is to eliminate an alternative as soon as it becomes clear that it has little chance of becoming the final selection. You may be able to select the best alternative after a single CBA, or it may be more cost-effective to use two or more passes at the alternatives, discarding the worst alternatives on the basis of preliminary cost and benefit data, and developing improved cost and benefit data for the remaining alternatives.

Remember not to spend more resources performing analysis than the value you expect to gain from the resulting information.

For example, suppose your task is to select the thickest of several metal plates while spending the least money possible measuring the plates. Assume you can measure very roughly with the naked eye for free, you can measure fairly accurately with a tape measure for $1 per plate, and you can measure precisely with a micrometer for $4 per plate (see **Exhibit 5-1**). Using eyesight alone, eliminate as many plates as possible from further consideration. This equates to eliminating some alternatives informally during the process design stage. Next, use the tape measure to identify which of the remaining alternatives might be the largest, and those which clearly are not. Finally, use a micrometer, the most accurate but also most expensive measurement tool, to pick the thickest plate from the last group of alternatives.

Conducting a CBA in a similar manner is often a cost-effective approach. The initial, less precise evaluations are analogous to the preliminary Functional Economic Analysis (FEA) that DoD recommends during the course of a BPR effort. The more precise measurement with the micrometer is analogous to the final FEA.

Consider the following when determining the level of analysis required for selecting among alternatives in a CBA:

Exhibit 5-1 Eliminate obvious alternatives using the least expensive methods.

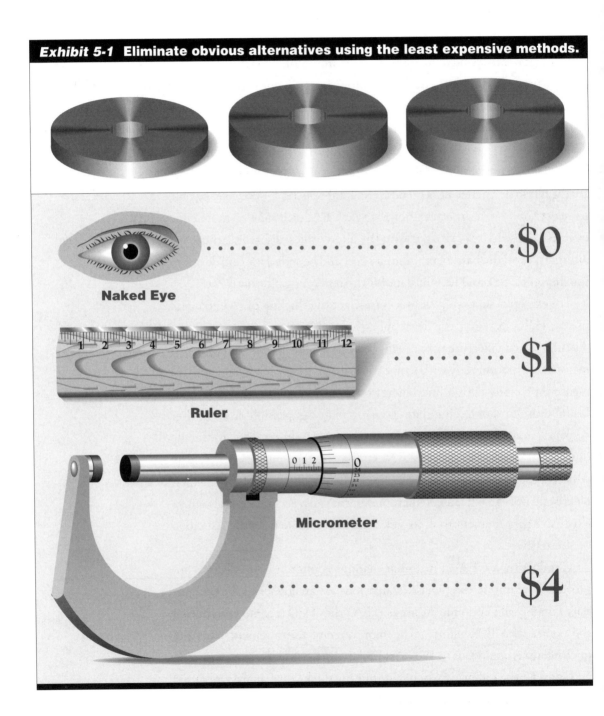

Naked Eye $0

Ruler $1

Micrometer

.... $4

- Availability of cost and benefit data
- Cost of developing more detailed cost and benefit data
- Cost of making an incorrect decision

This is the approach generally recommended by DoD. DoD also states that only a single FEA is necessary in some cases.

ESTIMATE COSTS AND BENEFITS FOR EACH ALTERNATIVE

Begin the selection process by developing initial costs and benefits for the alternatives to be evaluated in your CBA. This process involves assessing the impacts (including required investment costs) of process changes and estimating To-Be activity costs. Keep in mind that after estimating To-Be activity costs, it is necessary to eliminate any extra resources to realize savings. Adjust your budget for process reengineering savings by eliminating unnecessary resources or transferring resources to other uses.

Estimate costs and benefits for each alternative by examining the resources, inputs, and outputs of your To-Be activity models.

The return on investment calculated by the CBA takes into consideration only financial, or quantifiable, costs and benefits. Try to quantify non-financial costs and benefits in financial terms so that you can document their impact in your analysis. Aspects of the proposed alternative that are not quantified in financial terms cannot contribute to the alternative's worthiness in terms of return on investment. Use the following guidelines when quantifying non-financial costs and benefits:

- Record all assumptions
- Do not make assumptions that you cannot reasonably defend in the context of your analysis
- Balance the inaccuracies resulting from assumptions with the cost of analysis you would need to prove your assumptions

Because the purpose of the CBA is to select the most advantageous alternative from an economic standpoint, you only need to demonstrate that the preferred alternative is: (1) the best alternative in terms of its financial impact; and (2) meets the requirements for return on investment. Use the CBA to record any additional non-financial benefits, but do not attempt to force financial quantifiers where they are not needed to arrive at the selection decision. It is more important to treat all alternatives

Aspects of the proposed alternative that are not quantified in financial terms cannot contribute to the alternative's worthiness in terms of return on investment.

equally, equitably, and consistently, a task that becomes even more challenging when non-financial aspects are brought into the picture.

Assess the Impacts of Process Changes

To-Be IDEF0 activity models provide the basis for performing a CBA of your alternatives. To assess costs and benefits, you should examine the impacts of process changes on three of the four parts of the activity model: resources (mechanisms), inputs, and outputs. You do not need to consider impacts of process change on controls in the activity models, because these impacts are ultimately reflected in changes in resources, inputs, and outputs. Types of costs and benefits associated with resources, inputs, and outputs are illustrated in **Exhibit 5-2**.

Exhibit 5-2 All IDEF0 components except Controls map to the CBA.		
	Costs	**Benefits**
Resource (Mechanism)	One-time investiment costs (capital investments)	Income from salvage of prior capital investments
	Recurring (operational) costs	Savings from foregone investments required by status quo
		Recurring (operational) cost savings
Inputs	Available input volume, quality, cycle time, etc. inadequate to meet process needs	Decreased need for input volume, quality, cycle time, etc.
Output	Degraded output volume, quality, cycle time, etc.	Improved output volume, quality, cycle time, etc.

Resource Impacts

Resource impacts are caused by changes in resource consumption and include the benefits of cost savings (due to reduced resource consumption) and the additional costs (resulting from increased resource consumption). Typical resource impacts to consider include the following:

- *Expenditures for capital investments:* Capital investments include new equipment, facilities, personnel, information technology, etc., and are made throughout a program's life cycle. For example, capital investments in nuclear waste storage facilities may occur many years after the initial procurement of nuclear reactors and other generators of nuclear waste. Determining these costs is usually straightforward once you identify the needed investments.

- *Income from salvage:* Process changes may eliminate the need for capital purchased in a previous investment. For example, new processes or technology may eliminate the need for older equipment, which you can then sell for salvage.

- *Savings from avoiding investments:* Investing in an alternative may eliminate the need to invest in resources that the As-Is processes would otherwise have required. For example, upgrades to a no longer adequate computer system would be avoided by purchasing a newer system that incorporates those features. Cost avoidance is a tricky issue, however, and should be used in a CBA only when the investment is absolutely necessary in order to continue conducting the process, or more ideally when it is already built into current projections.

- *Savings from eliminating/simplifying old activities:* Eliminated activities no longer consume resources. Simplifying activities, or making them more efficient, reduces operational costs. The resulting cost savings are a benefit.

- *New and/or increased activity costs:* Process changes may consume additional resources and therefore increase costs for certain existing activities, or add costs for new activities. These costs differ from investment costs, because they are associated with changing the on-going activities of your organization. Consequently, the cost of new activities may continue indefinitely. Use ABC&P as a tool to determine these activity costs.

Typical resource impacts to consider include expenditures for capital investment; income from salvage; savings from avoiding investments; savings from eliminating and simplifying old activities; and new and/or increased activity costs.

Input Impacts

Input impacts are the financial and non-financial effects of process changes on inputs required from suppliers. Suppliers may be internal (e.g., another activity) or external (e.g., a vendor) to the activity model. A change to an activity in a To-Be model alternative may positively or negatively affect the input requirements of the activity in terms of availability, performance, specifications, etc. Different input requirements may in turn impact the resource consumption of and therefore the costs to the supplier. If the supplier is internal to the activity model (i.e., an earlier activity), the changes in cost would be reflected in the cost of the supplying activity. If the supplier is external to the activity model, the changes in cost would be reflected in changes to the costs of the inputs (e.g., raw materials or other vendor-supplied products) to the current activity.

Output Impacts

Output impacts include all non-financial impacts of an activity or group of activities, including performance, quality, and cycle time. Positive output impacts may be the objective of your BPR initiative, or a secondary result. Negative output impacts are identified as costs in a CBA and have the potential of undermining your BPR effort. Evaluate these outputs carefully. Understanding the economic impact of outputs through a CBA, can help you justify proposed process changes.

Estimate To-Be Activity Costs

Understanding approximate To-Be activity costs is essential in determining the best alternatives to analyze in more detail. Various techniques

ASSESSING THE IMPACTS OF PROCESS CHANGE

Chris and her team evaluated several approaches for automating the tracking of repair orders and telephones during the maintenance process. They built a detailed activity model for each of the best candidate alternatives, reflecting how the activities would be linked if that particular alternative were implemented. The team considered only those activities that would be affected by BPR, either in terms of performance or cost.

To cost the new models, the team identified all new processes, all eliminated processes, processes that either increased or decreased in activity level, and any other on-going expenditures or savings. For one alternative, they identified the following results:

- The activity "Forward Repair Order to Data Processing" would be eliminated
- The activity "Enter Repair Order" was eliminated
- The activity "Forward to Shipping" would be reduced by 20%
- The activity "Track Repair Orders" would be reduced by 35%

exist for estimating the costs of To-Be activities. ABC&P is one technique that provides a very accurate estimate. However, you only need to use ABC&P when that degree of accuracy is needed to eliminate alternatives. Other cost estimating techniques such as extrapolation, prototyping, and parametric analysis may be sufficient to arrive at rough estimates for To-Be activity costs. Use the estimating techniques that provide the best information given the level of detail required. The remainder of this section discusses how to use ABC&P for estimating the cost of To-Be activities.

A good place to start is by comparing your To-Be activity models with the As-Is model. For example, some activities in your To-Be model will be unchanged from the As-Is model (same resources, products, drivers, volume, etc.). The costs of these activities can be drawn from the cost of the activities in the As-Is model. Other activities may be similar to those in your As-Is model. For these, use whatever relationships and cost information from your As-Is model as appropriate to expedite your analysis.

For To-Be activities that are not in your As-Is model, you will need to develop new cost estimates. Use your IDEF0 activity models as the basis for further defining the resources, activities, products, and the relationships among these components in your To-Be activities to be costed. The amount of detail in each resulting ABC&P model should be limited to that necessary for differentiating among alternatives. Calculating the costs of the To-Be activities requires reversing the usual steps used in calculating As-Is costs. Begin the process with an understanding of customer requirements. Use this knowledge to estimate the volume of products required by customers. Then use the volume to estimate the activity level necessary to produce the required types and quantities of products. Finally, use this information to estimate planned resource consumption.

The amount of detail in each ABC&P model should be limited to that necessary for differentiating among alternatives.

The approach outlined above is a bottom-up approach because it involves estimating the costs for each activity and then adding them together to arrive at the cost for the To-Be process alternative. Another way is to calculate the difference between each To-Be alternative and the As-Is model. This also involves comparing To-Be activities with As-Is activities, but now you must also account for As-Is activities that are eliminated in the To-Be alternative.

For example, suppose the local government travel office is instituting electronic filing of travel vouchers. This process change will add several activities and eliminate others. Assume last year's transaction volume was 15,000 vouchers. Assume also that next year's volume is estimated at 15,000 vouchers, but approximately 10,000 of the vouchers will be filed electronically. A significant activity in processing travel vouchers in the current model is "Record Traveler Information." This activity involves entering information including the names, Social Security Numbers, and units of assignment into an electronic database. This activity will be largely eliminated after implementing electronic filing, as the travelers will enter this data themselves when they fill out their travel vouchers. Assume that the As-Is ABC&P model shows the "Record Traveler Information" activity cost $37,500 to operate last year for the 15,000 travel vouchers that were processed. The cost to perform this activity one time, called the activity driver rate, was therefore:

$$\frac{\$37,500 \,/\, \text{year}}{15,000 \text{ vouchers processed/year}} = \$2.50 \text{ per voucher processed}$$

A quick way to estimate savings from eliminating part or all of an activity is to multiply the activity driver rate times the reduction in the number of times the activity is performed. In the above case, the estimated reduction of the occurrences of the activity "Record Traveler Information" is 10,000. The estimated savings would therefore be:

10,000 x $2.50 = $25,000

The accuracy of this simplified approach to estimating savings is dependent on the degree actual costs are reflected in the driver used (in this case, the number of vouchers processed) and whether all costs are assigned to the activity cost pool. If costs are allocated (rather than traced), the accuracy of the data is diminished. Furthermore, the costs of certain activities (e.g., sustaining activities) are not assigned to the activity cost pool, yet they may be changed by the new process and, over the long-term, may have cost implications.

To illustrate the limitation of allocation versus tracing, consider the prior example. Assume the following:

- Information technology support costs were allocated to the "Record Traveler Information" activity based on the number of persons in the activity.
- Overall information technology support costs were $8,000 per year for a 20-person travel accounting office.
- The "Record Traveler Information" activity required one person one-half time.

Given this information, the information technology support costs allocated to "Record Traveler Information" would be the total cost for the year of information technology support times the proportion of those resources used by the "Record Traveler Information" activity, or:

$$\$8,000 \times (1/2)/20 \ = \ \$200.$$

QUANTIFYING COST SAVINGS FOR A TO-BE ALTERNATIVE

Chris and her team then quantified the financial impacts of the above changes to processes, and also calculated monthly costs as follows:

Activity	As-Is Cost	To-Be Cost	Savings
Forward RO to Data Processing	$400	$0	$400
Enter Repair Order	8221	0	8221
Forward to Shipping	8233	6586	1647
Track Repair Orders	5333	3466	1867
Total Savings			$12,135

To implement the above To-Be model, additional information technology would also be required. Currently Chris's facility leases their personal computers and covers them with a maintenance contract. Recurring costs for the computers and maintenance rental were expected to increase by 20%.

Resource	As-Is Cost	To-Be Cost	Added Cost
Information Technology	$1765	$2118	$353

The net savings resulting from this alternative would be as follows: process cost savings of $12,135 less additional information technology expenses of $353 equals a net savings of $11,782

However, because these costs are allocated and not traced, they may or may not be proportional to a reduction in the number of times that traveler information is recorded. A 2/3 reduction in the number of vouchers processed through the activity may therefore not result in a 2/3 reduction in the usage of information technology support.

Although this example highlights a limitation of ABC&P, the accuracy of the information is still likely to be better than if traditional cost estimating techniques are used.

COMPARE COSTS AND BENEFITS OF ALTERNATIVES TO THE AS-IS

In a CBA the As-Is model is the baseline against which other alternatives are measured.

The next step in selecting an alternative is comparing the costs and benefits of each To-Be alternative to your As-Is model. The As-Is model is always an alternative for a CBA because it is the baseline against which you measure the cost savings for the other alternatives. It is important to understand the cost and performance drivers of the baseline so that you can assess the progress of your BPR project after you have selected and implemented changes. Because the To-Be model looks to the future, the As-Is model must be extended to reflect forecasted changes in demand and previously planned process changes and investments. Comparisons between To-Be alternatives and the extended As-Is must use a common basis of inflation, risk, and time. For example, one alternative may start producing results immediately, have most of its investment costs in future years, and entail very little risk. An opposing alternative may require all investment at the beginning, require several years to attain objectives, and entail significant risk. Comparing two alternatives while ignoring the risk or timing of costs and benefits might easily lead to the wrong choice.

SELECT THE BEST ALTERNATIVE

The next step is to select the best alternative. To make the right choice, first evaluate the financial analysis of each alternative, add the relevant non-financial information, and use your experience and judgment to choose the best alternative. This involves evaluating the costs and benefits defined for each alternative against defined selection criteria. Eliminate the alternatives that do not meet the defined selection criteria. For example, if the cost of an alternative exceeds the available funding, eliminate it from further consideration. Selection criteria are the discriminators for decision making. Choose criteria that highlight meaningful differences among alternatives. For example, assume you are required to produce 500 widgets a day, and that all alternatives under consideration are able to meet this requirement. The ability to produce 500 widgets a day is therefore not a discriminator for selecting one alternative over another, regardless of its importance. However, the ability to produce 500 widgets of greater quality or at lower cost are unequal factors among alternatives and may be discriminators for choosing one alternative over its competitors.

Selection criteria are the discriminators for decision making. Choose criteria that highlight meaningful differences among alternatives.

SUMMARY

Performing a CBA helps you select your new business practices. The objective of a CBA is to help you discriminate between the best alternative and all others, and evaluate whether that alternative provides a minimum required return on investment. ABC&P is a useful tool in accomplishing this objective for the following reasons: ABC&P provides you with accurate historical costs that serve as a basis for accurate cost estimating; ABC&P can be performed in reverse order to estimate activity costs for your To-Be models; and the modeling and performance aspects of ABC&P force you to consider how changes to one activity impact the other activities in a process, ensuring you consider these impacts in your analysis. You can then estimate and compare the costs and benefits of alternatives to your As-Is model and use pre-defined selection criteria to choose the best alternative.

The specific approach for performing a CBA endorsed by DoD is the FEA. If your CBA must meet DoD guidelines, use the specific procedures outlined in the *FEA Guidebook* in performing your CBA. Integrating the concepts presented in this chapter into FEAs will result in FEAs that reflect the activity-based insights vital to BPR initiatives.

CHAPTER 1

CHAPTER 2

CHAPTER 3

CHAPTER 4

CHAPTER 5

CHAPTER 6

ABC Performance

Making
Improvements
Succeed

Now this is not the end. It is not even the beginning of the end. But it is, perhaps, the end of the beginning.

– *SIR WINSTON CHURCHILL*

CHAPTER 6: MAKING IMPROVEMENTS SUCCEED

BPR projects often fail because efforts stop after the To-Be process model has been selected and investments made. You can ensure long-term benefits from BPR by including the following steps in your effort:

- Formalize new processes
- Fine tune reengineered processes
- Lock in BPR gains
- Reimplement BPR as necessary

FORMALIZE NEW PROCESSES

Implementing a To-Be model requires more than simply selecting an alternative and making the necessary investment. Formalize the new processes so that all participants can understand and consistently execute them. This involves doing the following:

- Define detailed specifications and procedures for new processes
- Motivate and train personnel
- Establish a new organizational structure

Formalizing new business processes helps process participants understand and execute them consistently.

Define Detailed Specifications and Procedures for New Processes

Carefully documenting process specifications and procedures establishes a common point of reference for understanding, communicating, and executing new processes.

Capture the insights you gained from activity modeling and ABC&P analysis by documenting process specifications and procedures. These specifications and procedures provide a common point of reference that will enable managers to better understand, communicate, and execute the processes in a consistent manner over time.

They also help you establish an "expectations baseline" against which you can track implementation progress. By measuring results achieved at any point in time against those expected, you will be able to identify sources of discrepancies and take corrective action. You can further ensure progress by specifying process requirement expectations over time during implementation. For example, if you are implementing a BPR project in multiple phases, specify expectations for each phase, and evaluate your progress against these expectations. You can also set goals for future process performance to encourage continual process improvement after the initial reengineering effort is complete.

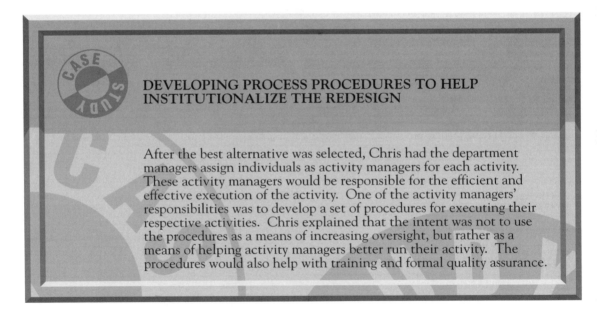

CASE STUDY

DEVELOPING PROCESS PROCEDURES TO HELP INSTITUTIONALIZE THE REDESIGN

After the best alternative was selected, Chris had the department managers assign individuals as activity managers for each activity. These activity managers would be responsible for the efficient and effective execution of the activity. One of the activity managers' responsibilities was to develop a set of procedures for executing their respective activities. Chris explained that the intent was not to use the procedures as a means of increasing oversight, but rather as a means of helping activity managers better run their activity. The procedures would also help with training and formal quality assurance.

Motivate and Train Personnel

Specifying process specifications and procedures in writing is a good start to successfully implementing reengineered processes, but it is not enough. Participating employees must also change their behavior. People can either enable or obstruct progress of cost and performance improvements. Make sure all participating employees are motivated and trained in the reengineered processes.

You can motivate people by making sure they understand the need for change, realize they have an important role in the reengineered process, and feel their needs and concerns have been considered during the reengineering effort. Involving employees throughout the effort helps accomplish this, and also allows you to take advantage of their expertise in the work they perform. Training helps you explain to them the need for change and provides them with the skills to execute the reengineered processes.

Establish a New Organizational Structure

Through BPR you determine *what* you need to accomplish (your corporate goals and objectives), and then define *how* you can best attain those goals and objectives. You must also address your organizational structure to reflect *who* is to perform the processes. A well designed organizational structure that is aligned and congruent with the reengineered processes will help ensure the stability and success of those processes. Activities and individual work efforts are well aligned with the organizational structure when they support corporate goals. Alignment is an important enabler of making an organization effective and efficient. To achieve alignment, establish an organizational structure that minimizes the number of conflicts and tradeoffs that arise in an organization as employees work to meet corporate goals. Your goal is to establish an organizational structure where remaining tradeoffs can be resolved at the lowest organizational level possible. This prevents the added inefficiencies of coordination among multiple management levels.

New processes require a new organizational structure. Organizational structures that are aligned and congruent with new business processes will ensure the stability and success of those processes.

After reengineering processes, assign responsibility for performing activities to the appropriate element of the organization, making the processes congruent with the organization. Each activity must have a specific organizational element responsible for its execution, and no organizational elements should perform work not defined as an activity. Without clear assignment of responsibility, a process in which everyone is in charge will become a process with no one in charge. Assigning responsibility makes individuals responsible for group goals and greatly increases the likelihood that you will attain expected improvements in performance and cost.

FINE TUNE REENGINEERED PROCESSES

Making minor adjustments to your reengineered process after monitoring initial results will help optimize your return on investment.

After selecting and implementing the appropriate To-Be model, closely monitor the initial operation of the reengineered processes and fine tune the processes as necessary. You make investments in the new model with the expectation that you will receive a return on these investments. You may need to make minor adjustments to processes to achieve the improvements and cost savings you originally envisioned. These include procedural changes to processes, additional changes to controls, and adjustments for unforeseen impacts on other processes. If such fine tuning does not bring your achievements in line with expectations, the assumptions on which the original analysis was conducted may have been flawed or made out-of-date by changes beyond the control of the BPR effort. In such an event, you may need to reevaluate to see if the reengineered processes you selected are still the best. If not, consider a subsequent reengineering effort.

LOCK IN BPR GAINS

Your BPR project is not complete until you have established an environment capable of self-sustainment. Lock in the gains from BPR for your organization. You may find it easier to identify the actions that will contribute to locking in gains by looking at cost and performance separately even though the two are intimately linked. The following techniques can help you lock in gains and ensure your organization does not go back to the old processes and business practices:

- Align culture with new business practices
- Establish a system for measuring BPR results
- Align performance measures with new business practices
- Initiate a program for continuous improvement

Align Culture With New Business Practices

The culture of an organization is reflected in the values and attitudes of both the managers and workers within the organization. Every organization has a culture. Some organizations encourage entrepreneurship and innovation, while others discourage risk taking. Some respond quickly to change, while others encourage stability. New processes usually require a change in an organization's culture.

You can implement change in the culture of your organization only with sufficient commitment by both managers and workers. The need for cultural change depends on the cultural requirements of the reengineered processes. Do the new processes require employees to work faster? Are workers expected to make decisions in situations in which they previously had no authority?

These and similar questions identify areas of misalignment between reengineered processes and organizational culture. To align culture and process, you need an environment of open communication and trust. One way to accomplish this is to provide training for managers and workers to explain the need for change, the plan for implementing changes, and the implications for the organization. Start this training during the design phase and continue it through implementation.

Establish a System for Measuring BPR Results

To adequately monitor the progress of your BPR effort, you need to compare projected cost savings with actual cost savings. An activity-based cost collection and reporting system is an ideal tool for monitoring progress, and can also help you update your original savings projections. Though directives and law place many requirements on DoD accounting systems, you can still establish an on-going activity-based cost collection and reporting system at the functional level. This system may require additional data collection. Automation, however, has greatly reduced the cost of data collection so most likely the benefits you gain from the additional cost insight will quickly exceed the cost of collecting additional data.

ABC&P is an ideal tool for measuring BPR results.

The projections you included in the cost-benefit analysis were based on assumptions made at the time the analysis was performed. New, up-to-date cost information will help you reflect changes in customer requirements, operating conditions, etc., so that you can accurately demonstrate the financial achievements of your BPR effort or make adjustments where necessary. When evaluating updated cost and performance data, you may also find new opportunities for improvement. Having the appropriate data at your fingertips will allow you to perform ABC&P analysis of these opportunities with very little cost and effort. Other areas of your organization may also benefit from cost and performance information. The Epilogue discusses activity-based cost collection and reporting systems in more detail.

ESTABLISHING AN ON-GOING ABC&P SYSTEM

Chris was happy to get one-time insights from ABC&P. However, she did not want to revert to relying solely on the company's traditional cost accounting system for all of her cost information now that the redesign effort was over. She decided to establish an on-going activity-based cost collection and reporting system to provide this information. The company controller had established a policy that all divisions would use the same accounting system and accounting software. Chris decided she would attempt to influence the company controller into establishing an activity-based system throughout the company. Until this happened, however, Chris decided to set up an off-line cost collecting and reporting system to supplement her current accounting information.

Align Performance Measures with New Business Practices

Measuring the performance of your new processes is vital to determining whether they are operating as efficiently as possible and if they are achieving needed outcomes. Choose performance measures carefully to make sure they provide adequate insight into the effectiveness and efficiency of your processes and outputs. To accomplish this, take a customer's perspective. Good performance measures yield insight into the ability to cost-effectively meet the needs of both external customers (end users) and internal customers (customers of the process within the organization).

If you identify processes that do not operate as efficiently as you planned, or do not produce outcomes that meet your customers' requirements, analyze those processes in terms of operation, inputs, mechanisms, and controls to determine the cause of the problem. Also analyze the problem's impact on the cost and performance objectives of your BPR effort. Take corrective action to fix or reengineer processes as appropriate, and then reevaluate them against expectations.

Initiate Program for Continuous Improvement

After implementing all the improvements of your BPR effort, initiate a continuous process improvement program. The program will help ensure your organization's success by continuously finding ways of improving productivity, making it more likely to survive. Environments constantly change. Innovations in technology, new customer expectations, and other factors influence how effectively and efficiently your processes operate. Continuous process improvement enables you to adjust processes to changes in the environment without major costly overhauls.

REIMPLEMENT BPR AS NECESSARY

While a program of continuous process improvement typically delays the need for reengineering, sudden changes in the environment, or continued improvements that cost more than the benefits gained may require that your reengineered processes will again become candidates for reengineering. The environment can change in ways that preclude continuous process improvement from fully meeting the needs of customers. For example, continuously improving the process of filing documents in a filing cabinet would no longer be useful if your organization shifts to storing documents as digital images on an optical disk instead of on paper.

There is no single answer as to how often to reengineer, because the answer is dependent on many variables. How rapidly is your business environment changing (technology, government regulation, customer demands, etc.)? How widespread was the last BPR initiative? How aggressive is your competition? These and similar questions form the basis for determining the need for additional reengineering. In general, BPR is warranted if the processes in use can significantly benefit from it. Only good judgment applied to the organization in question can accurately answer the question of when to reengineer.

SUMMARY

Selecting and implementing an alternative To-Be model is not the final step in BPR. In fact, BPR can easily fail if you do not take necessary follow-up steps to ensure your newly designed processes are fully implemented and monitored. Formalizing your reengineered processes by defining specifications and procedures, motivating and training personnel, and establishing a new organizational structure will ensure that all participants can understand and consistently execute processes correctly. Fine tuning your reengineered processes by monitoring improvement progress will help you optimize your return on investment. Aligning your organization's culture, establishing a system for measuring BPR results, aligning performance measures, and initiating a continuous improvement program will lock in BPR gains and establish an environment capable of self-sustainment. Each of these actions will help your organization benefit from BPR and minimize the need to reengineer again. Eventually, however, circumstances beyond your control may require you to reengineer again to remain effective and competitive.

ABC
Performance

Epilogue:
What the Future
Holds

EPILOGUE - WHAT THE FUTURE HOLDS

ABC&P is a valuable tool for making wise investment decisions during BPR efforts. Yet ABC&P is capable of much more than helping to identify and select the best process improvement opportunities. ABC&P can also help you make better management decisions while operating within your new processes. This Epilogue introduces the following ways to use ABC&P as a general management tool:

- Step beyond cost analysis
- Improve cost collection and reporting
- Encourage strategic management
- Align budgets
- Maximize process management

STEP BEYOND COST ANALYSIS

As a manager, you are probably responsible for managing costs. As a part of BPR, you analyzed costs on a project by project, alternative by alternative basis. Cost management involves more than cost analysis. It involves

Effective cost management involves continuously aligning your expenses with your strategic goals and operational needs.

123

ongoing attention to resource consumption in a way that aligns your investment and recurring expenditures with both long-term (strategic) and short-term (operational) goals and objectives.

In addition to managing cost, you must manage processes. Process management involves tracking both the effectiveness and efficiency of processes. You can evaluate the effectiveness of a process based on its ability to satisfy customer needs. You can evaluate a process's efficiency by comparing its output (a product or service) with its inputs (resources).

Organizations committed to cost and process management have an ongoing need for ABC&P insight. While a one-time activity-based cost analysis may be valuable for improving investment decisions, it does little for managing costs and performance on a day-to-day basis. Resource consumption is not static. It varies because of predictable influences such as scheduled changes in production volume, and seasonal and budgetary cycles. It also varies because of unpredictable influences such as war or crises. ABC&P, implemented as an ongoing system, enables you to continuously evaluate and adjust your costs and processes.

IMPROVE COST COLLECTION AND REPORTING

Continuous activity-based cost collection provides a means of continuous improvement.

Establishing an activity-based cost collection and reporting[1] system allows you to monitor the progress of your BPR effort, update your savings projections if necessary, pinpoint additional BPR opportunities, and reduce the effort required for your next BPR or ABC&P project.

You can build your activity-based cost collection and reporting system by using the basic principles of ABC&P, incorporating repetitive cost measurement and reporting over time, and employing procedures and automation tools that quickly and efficiently trace costs to activities on an on-going basis.

Repetitive cost measurement requires a defined period for repeating cost collection and reporting. When defining this period, keep in mind influences such as changes in production volume, technology, cost measurement objectives (strategic vs. operational), and other factors that vary

---

[1] On-going activity-based cost collection and reporting is also known as activity-based accounting.

with time. Weigh the cost of collecting activity-based cost information against this defined reporting period. You can minimize this cost by developing and implementing procedures and automation tools to quickly compile and integrate information on activities, resources, and products and services provided. The time you save by reducing the level of effort required to repeatedly collect and report activity-based costs, and the resulting savings they may help identify, may justify your investment in these tools and procedures.

You can develop your cost collection and reporting system to be either an *on-line* or *off-line* system. An *on-line* system is an extension of an official accounting system. For an on-line system you may need to establish sub-accounts for the extension under existing accounts required by DoD 7200.1 and DoD 7220.9-M. You also need to establish a list of processes, activities, and sub-activities/tasks for the extension, and provide a means of linking tasks with the resources they consume.

An off-line system does not affect the procedures or automation tools in official accounting systems. For an off-line system, you need to establish a separate set of procedures and tools to take relevant data available from your official accounting system and supplement it with additional data as necessary to generate the required activity-based cost data.

The primary difference between the two approaches is that the on-line system closely integrates required accounting functions such as those mandated by Federal and DoD regulations with the activity-based cost functions, while the off-line approach treats the two independently. The advantage of the on-line approach is it creates a single cost system.

Whichever approach you choose, gain comptroller support early in the design and development process. Inform comptroller personnel about activity-based costing, your organization's specific needs and objectives for activity-based cost information, and system design considerations. Once comptroller personnel understand how you intend to use ABC&P, their experience and knowledge of the existing cost system will prove valuable in designing a new activity-based cost system. Failure to involve the comptroller community in areas in which they have responsibilities and interests can understandably lead to reluctance to endorse any system.

Gain comptroller support early in the process of setting up an activity-based cost collection and reporting system.

ENCOURAGE STRATEGIC MANAGEMENT

Cost information is essential for effective strategic management.

Many organizations within DoD are using strategic management to identify opportunities and challenges for the future. Strategic management will become even more widespread as the requirements of the *Government Performance and Results Act* are implemented over the next several years. Cost information is essential to effective strategic management. ABC&P provides the accurate cost information and insights needed.

You must consider the long-term impacts of controlling costs and making investments. Distinguish between investments that add strategic value, and those that add only cost. To get the most value from investments, focus investments on achieving strategic goals and tightly tie them to corporate strategies. Doing this involves *strategic cost management*. Strategic cost management consists of the following three elements:

1. Understanding the organization's true product costs
2. Ensuring resource allocations are aligned with key strategic goals
3. Analyzing the company's strategic costs against its best "competitors"

As discussed throughout this book, ABC&P is a valuable tool for accurately assessing product costs, meeting the needs of the first element of strategic cost management. To meet the second element, continue to evaluate your newly implemented ABC&P model to ensure that your activities continue to meet your customer's changing needs. Adjust your strategic plans to reflect this approach. To meet the third element of strategic cost management, use ABC&P data to evaluate the costs and performance of your activities in continued benchmarking (for setting new goals) and continued best practices analysis (to find ways to perform activities better).

ABC&P helps you identify the cost of performing your organization's significant activities with far more objectivity than traditional accounting systems. Also, the process view of ABC&P provides a convenient way of understanding and tracking the effectiveness and efficiency of activities. Finally, cost-benefit analyses conducted on the basis of activity-based cost information provide more accurate information about improvement initiatives.

ALIGN BUDGETS

Many DoD managers are used to thinking of budgets as bank accounts that they must empty each year or risk losing the balance. This attitude does not encourage the increasing efficiency necessary in today's budgetary environment.

Realistic budgets are a vital planning tool for all public and private organizations. ABC&P is a tool for setting realistic budgets. Budgets determine how much you can spend and where you can spend it, thus defining the limits of what your organization can do. Inaccurate budgets can therefore have substantial negative effects on your organization. An example of an unrealistic budget is one that does not allot resources adequately to accomplish assigned tasks.

ABC&P is useful in developing realistic, useful budgets by helping you accurately estimate the required output level of products and services based on customer needs rather than hopes or speculation. You can use the accurate output level to then estimate the corresponding activity level. You can then use the activity level to estimate realistic resource requirements.

Budgets based on activities are more accurate than those built by traditional methods because they are built on a clear understanding of what drives cost within an organization. They are more reliable because they are flexible. As conditions change during a budget cycle, you can quickly reflect changing customer demands for products and services in revised budget requirements. Just as importantly, revised budgets are more accurate for the same reasons original budgets are more accurate, enabling you to revise budgets less frequently.

MAXIMIZE PROCESS MANAGEMENT

ABC&P is useful for maximizing process management from an operational view by helping to motivate employees and innovate products. The following two examples are from real companies. They illustrate creative ways of using the insights from ABC&P in this manner.

A circuit board plant uses an activity-based cost collection and reporting system to collect the costs of scrap and rework within various activities. The system assigns those costs to the activity that caused the scrap or rework. This assigns the cost of poor quality to the activity that *caused* the defect, rather than the activity required to *fix* the defect. This cost system thus provides insight into the costs of poor quality, and encourages improved quality in activities that cause defects.

A computer hardware company provides another example of the innovative use of ABC&P. This company provides activity costs associated with using different types of electronic equipment components to its design engineers. As a result, these engineers can use this information to develop more cost effective product designs.

These are only two examples that illustrate how you can use ABC&P information on a daily basis to help improve your operations. Think of ways you can use ABC&P as a means of improving the cost effectiveness of decisions throughout your organization, even after your BPR effort is complete.

SUMMARY

The success of your organization depends on effective cost and process management on an on-going basis. ABC&P is a tool for accomplishing strategic cost management because it provides the strategic cost and performance information necessary for planning the future of your organization. ABC&P is also useful for developing more realistic, useful budgets, thereby giving you a tool for managing future costs. Finally, ABC&P is valuable as an operational tool by helping you make more cost-effective decisions on a day-to-day basis. As DoD implements ABC&P, it will become more cost-effective and efficient.

R E F E R E N C E S

A   B   C   &   P

Books

Ansoff, H.I., <u>The New Corporate Strategy</u>. New York, NY: John Wiley & Sons, 1987.

Barker, Joel. <u>Future Edge</u>. New York, NY: William Morrow and Company, Inc., 1992.

Bosomworth, Charles. <u>The Executive Benchmarking Guidebook</u>. Boston, MA: Management Roundtable, 1993.

Brassard, Michael. <u>The Memory Jogger Plus+</u>™. Methuen, MA: Goal/QPC, 1989.

Brimson, James A. <u>Activity Accounting: An Activity-Based Costing Approach</u>. New York, NY: John Wiley and Sons, Inc., 1991.

Cokins, Gary, Alan Stratton and Jack Helbling. <u>An ABC Manager's Primer</u>. Montvale, NJ: Institute of Management Accountants, 1993.

Cooper, Robin, Robert Kaplan, Lawrence Maisel, Eileen Morrissey, and Ronald Oehm. <u>Implementing Activity-Based Cost Management: Moving from Analysis to Action</u>. Montvale, NJ: Institute of Management Accountants, 1992.

D. Appleton Company, Inc. <u>Corporate Information Management: Process Improvement Methodology for DoD Functional Managers</u>. Fairfax, VA: D. Appleton Company, Inc., 1993.

Davenport, Thomas H. <u>Process Innovation: Reengineering Work through Information Technology</u>. Boston, MA: Harvard Business School Press, 1993.

Defense Investigative Service. <u>Functional Economic Analysis Foundation Workshop</u>. Washington, D. C.: Defense Investigative Service and D. Appleton Company, Inc., 1992.

Gore, Albert. <u>From Red Tape to Results: Creating a Government that Works Better & Costs Less</u>. Washington, D.C.: U.S. Government Printing Office, 1993.

Hammer, Michael and James Champy. <u>Reengineering the Corporation: A Manifesto for Business Revolution</u>. New York, NY: Harper Business, 1993.

Johnson, H. Thomas and Robert S. Kaplan. <u>Relevance Lost: The Rise and Fall of Management Accounting</u>. Boston, MA: Harvard Business School Press, 1991.

Katzenbach, Jon R. and Douglas K. Smith. <u>The Wisdom of Teams, Creating the High-Performance Organization</u>. Boston, MA: Harvard Business School Press, 1993.

Office of the Secretary of Defense, Director of Defense Information. <u>Functional Process Improvement (Functional Management Process for Improving the Information Management Program of the Department of Defense) 8020.1-M (Draft)</u>. Washington, D.C.: Office of the Secretary of Defense, 1992.

Office of the Secretary of Defense, Director of Defense Information. <u>Functional Economic Analysis Guidebook</u>. Washington, D.C.: Office of the Secretary of Defense, 1991.

Office of the Deputy Assistant Secretary of Defense for Total Quality Management. <u>Total Quality Management Guide</u>. Washington, D.C.: Department of Defense, 1990.

Ostrenga, Michael R., Terrence R. Ozan, Robert D. McIlhattan, and Marcus D. Harwood. <u>The Ernst & Young Guide to Total Cost Management</u>. New York, NY: John Wiley and Sons, Inc., 1992.

R E F E R E N C E S

A   B   C   &   P

Books (cont'd)

Porter, Michael. Competitive Strategy: Creating and Sustaining Superior Performance. New York, NY: Free Press, Inc., 1985.

Porter, Michael. Competitive Strategy: Techniques for Analyzing Industries and Company. New York, NY: Free Press, Inc., 1980.

The CAM-I Glossary of Activity-Based Management, Edited by Norm Raffish and Peter B.B Turney, (Arlington: CAM-I, 1991)

Turney, Peter B.B. Common Cents. Hillsboro, OR: Cost Technology, 1992.

United States Department of Defense. Comptroller of the Department of Defense. Key Criteria for Performance Measurement. Washington, D.C.: U.S. Dept. of Defense, 1992.

United States Department of Defense. Office of the Assistant Secretary for Defense (Comptroller). Department of Defense Accounting Manual 7220.9 M. Washington, D.C.: Office of the Assistant Secretary for Defense (Comptroller), 1988.

Articles

Bernowski, Karen. "The Benchmarking Bandwagon." Quality Progress January. 1991: 19-24.

Camp, Robert C. "Benchmarking: The Search for Best Practices that Lead to Superior Performance Part I." Quality Progress January. 1989: 61-68.

Camp, Robert C. "Benchmarking: The Search for Industry Best Practices that Lead to Superior Performance Part III." Quality Progress March. 1989: 76-82.

Cooper, Robin. "The Rise of Activity Based Costing-Part Four: What do Activity-Based Cost Systems Look Like?" Harvard Business Review Spring 1989: 38-49.

Cooper, Robin. "The Rise of Activity-Based Costing-Part One: What is an Activity-Based Cost System?" Harvard Business Review Summer 1988: 45-54.

Cooper, Robin. "The Rise of Activity-Based Costing-Part Three: How many cost drivers do you need, and how do you select them?" Harvard Business Review Winter 1989: 34-45.

Cooper, Robin. "The Rise of Activity-Based Costing-Part Two: When do I need an Activity-Based Cost System?" Harvard Business Review Fall 1988: 41-48.

Cooper, Robin. "You need a New Cost System When..." Harvard Business Review January-February 1989: 77-82.

Cooper, Robin and Robert S. Kaplan. "Measure Costs Right: Make the Right Decisions." Harvard Business Review September-October 1988: 96 -103.

Gardner, John W. "The Nature of Leadership." The Independent Sector January 1986: 8.

MacArthur, John B. "Activity-Based Costing: How Many Cost Drivers Do You Want?" Journal of Cost Management Fall 1992: 37-41.

McDonald, Kelly K. "The Use of IDEF0 in Activity-Based Costing: Evaluating the Costs of doing Business in a Service Industry." IDEF-Users Group Conference Proceedings October 1992.

A   B   C   &   P

Articles (cont'd)

Miller, John A. "Designing and Implementing a New Cost System." <u>Journal of Cost Management</u> Winter 1992: 41-53.

Moravec, Robert D. and Michael S. Yoemans. "Using ABC to Support Business Re-Engineering in the Department of Defense." <u>Journal of Cost Management</u> Summer 1992: 32-41.

Pirrong, Gordon D. "As Easy as ABC." <u>The National Public Accountant</u> February 1993: 22-26.

Rotch, William. "Activity-Based Costing in Service Industries." <u>Journal of Cost Management</u> Summer 1990: 4-14.

Sharman, Paul A. "Activity-Based Management: A Growing Practice." <u>CMA Magazine</u> March 1993: 17-22.

Vaziri, H. Kevin. "Using Competitive Benchmarking to Set Goals." <u>Quality Progress</u> October 1992: 81-85.

Webster, Douglas W. "Activity-Based Costing Facilitates Concurrent Engineering." <u>Concurrent Engineering: Issues, Technologies, and Practice</u>. November/December 1991: 10-18.

Bills

U.S. Senate. <u>Government Performance and Results Act of 1993</u>. 103rd Cong., 1st sess., S. 20.

U.S. Congress. House. <u>Chief Financial Officers Act of 1990</u>. 101st Cong., 2nd sess., H.R. 5687.

Dissertation

Webster, Douglas W. "The Use of Activity Accounting for Improving Investment Management in the Manufacturing Firm: Three Case Studies." DBA Dissertation. U.S. International University, San Diego, California, 1990.

Personal Interviews

Oswalt, Leo, BPI Division, U.S. Army Center for Public Works, Ft. Belvoir, Virginia. Personal Interview. 22 September 1993.

Melroy, Russ, Defense General Supply Center, Richmond, Virginia. Personal Interview. 20 September 1993.

A   B   C   &   P

Cost Analysis
Layard, Richard. Cost Benefit Analysis. New York: Penguin Modern Economics Readings, 1972.

Oxenfeldt, Alfred Richard. Cost-Benefit Analysis for Executive Decision Making. New York, NY: AMACOM, 1979.

Shim, Jae K. and Joel G. Siegel. Modern Cost Management and Analysis. Italy: Barron's Educational Series, 1992.

Gulledge, Thomas R., William P. Hurtzler, and Joan S. Lovelace, Editors. Cost Estimating and Analysis. New York, NY: Springer-Verlag, 1992.

Business Process Reengineering
Bankes, Frank W., Kurt C. Doehnert, and Leif C. Ulstrup. "Taking AIM at Innovation." Federal Managers Quarterly Issue 3, 1993: 8-12.

Brassard, Michael. The Memory Jogger Plus+™. Methuen, MA: Goal/QPC, 1989.

Davenport, Thomas H. Process Innovation: Reengineering Work through Information Technology. Boston, MA: Harvard Business School Press, 1993.

Hammer, Michael and James Champy. Reengineering the Corporation: A Manifesto for Business Revolution. New York, NY: Harper Business, 1993.

Marca, D.A. and C.L. McGowan. SADT Structured Analysis and Design Technique™. New York, NY: McGraw Hill, 1988.

Osborne, David and Ted Gaebler. Reinventing Government: How the Entrepreneurial Spirit is Transforming the Public Sector. Reading, MA: Addison-Wesley Publishing Company, Inc., 1992.

Watson, Gregory H. The Benchmarking Workbook. Cambridge, MA: Productivity Press, 1992.

Project Management & Leadership
Cleland, D. I. and W.R. King. Project Management Handbook. New York: Van Nostrand and Rheinhold Company, 1988.

DePree, Max. Leadership is an Art. New York: Dell Publishing, 1989.

Katzenbach, Jon R. and Douglas K. Smith. "The Discipline of Teams." Harvard Business Review March-April 1993.

Katzenbach, Jon R., and Douglas K. Smith. The Wisdom of Teams. Boston, MA: Harvard Business School Press, 1993.

Kerzner, Harold. Project Management: a System Approach to Planning, Scheduling & Controlling. New York: Van Nostrand and Rheinhold Company, 1979.

Kerzner, Harold. Project Management for Executives. New York: Van Nostrand and Rheinhold Company, 1989.

Livingston, J. Sterling. "Pygmalion in Management." Harvard Business Review July/August 1969: 81-89.

A   B   C   &   P

Project Management & Leadership (cont'd)

Shultz, John and Robert Luby. "Reengineering and Reinventing the U.S. Naval Shipyards." Project Management Institutes' pmnetwork. February 1994: 15-25.

Struckenbruch, Linn C. The Implementation of Project Management: The Professional's Handbook. New York, NY: Addision Wesley Publishers, Inc., 1981.

Data Collection

Babbie, Earl R. Survey Research Methods. Belmont, California: Wadsworth Publishing Company, Inc., 1973.

Backstrom, Charles Herbert and Gerald D. Hursh. Survey Research. Chicago: Northwestern University Press, 1963.

Dexter, Lewis Anthony. Elite and Specialized Interviewing. Evanston, Illinois: Northwestern University Press, 1970.

Rea, Louis M. and Richard A. Parker. Designing and Conducting Survey Research: A Comprehensive Guide. San Francisco: Jossey-Bass Publishers, 1992.

Rosenberg, Morris. The Logic of Survey Analysis. New York: Basic Books, Inc., 1968.

Webb, Eugene J. Unobtrusive Measures; Nonreactive Research in the Social Sciences. Chicago: Rand McNally, 1966.

Strategic and Quality Management

Ansoff, H.I., The New Corporate Strategy. New York, NY: John Wiley & Sons, 1987.

Crosby, Philip B. Quality Without Tears: The Art of Hassle Free Management. New York: McGraw-Hill Book Company, 1984.

Porter, Michael. Competitive Strategy: Creating and Sustaining Superior Performance. New York, NY: Free Press, Inc., 1985.

Shank, John K. and Vijay Govindarajan. Strategic Cost Management. New York, NY: The Free Press, 1993.

Walton, Mary. The Deming Management Method. New York: Putnam Publishing Group, 1986.

United States General Accounting Office. Program Performance Measures: Federal Agency Collection and Use of Performance Data. Report # GAO/GGD-92-65.

[Activity] one step within a process that uses resources to perform work. It occurs over time (has a clear beginning and end) and has recognizable results.

[Activity Cost Pool] all cost elements associated with an activity and their total cost.

[Activity Driver] a measure of the frequency of activity performance and the effort required to achieve the end result.

[Activity Model] graphical representation of the activities that compose a business process, the flow of information and objects used and created by these activities, and the resources consumed by the activities.

[Allocation] the assignment of resource costs to activities or activity costs to products through apportionment or distribution; used when a direct measure of resource consumption or activity usage does not exist.

[Alternatives] "a slate of initiatives that can achieve a functional process' intended TO-BE state" (*Functional Economic Analysis Guidebook*).

[As-Is Model] a graphical representation of how a business process is currently being performed.

[Benchmarking] an analytical tool that involves measuring the performance of activities against the performance of similar activities in internal and external organizations considered to be the "best of the best."

[Best Practices Analysis] an analytical tool that involves learning how industry leaders perform activities with purposes similar to yours and adapting these practices to your organization to achieve superior performance.

[Bill of Activities] listing of all primary activities performed to produce a given product and their associated costs.

[Bill of Costs] a break-out of the specific cost elements within a cost pool for an activity.

[Business Process Reengineering] a disciplined approach for fundamentally redesigning an enterprise to achieve dramatic improvements in business performance.

[Cost Benefit Analysis] an analysis tool used to evaluate and compare the costs and benefits of alternative approaches to process reengineering.

[Cost Driver] an indicator of why an activity is performed and what causes the cost of performing the activity to change.

[Cost Element] each resource used by an activity and its associated cost.

[Cost Object] see Product.

[Dynamic Simulation] an abstract representation of a system, including the dimension of time, that is based on a set of assumptions and expressed as mathematical or logical relationship between objects.

[Functional Economic Analysis] "a management tool to determine and document the costs and benefits of business process improvements and related investments in information technology" (*Functional Economic Analysis Guidebook*).

A   B   C   &   P

[IDEFO] (pronounced eye-deaf-zero) process (activity) modeling technique developed in the 1970s by the U.S. Air Force and adopted by the Department of Defense Corporate Information Management (CIM) Technology Policy Board as the mandatory business process modeling technique.

[Interrelationship Diagraph] an exercise that helps identify all logical relationships among activities within a process.

[Metrics] methods used to perform business processes.

[Paradigm] a set of rules (written or unwritten) that establishes or defines boundaries and tells how to behave inside the boundaries to be successful (*The Future Edge*).

[Pareto Analysis] an analytical tool to identify high-cost activities; based on the 80/20 rule that 20 percent of what is done accounts for 80 percent of the cost.

[Performance Measure] "an indicator of the work performed and the results achieved in an activity" (*Common Cents*).

[Primary activity] an activity that contributes directly to a final product.

[Process] a group of activities performed to achieve a desired business objective(s).

[Product] any object about which you wish to gain financial or other information through cost and performance measurement.

[Resource] the elements (e.g., labor, materials, facilities) used to perform work.

[Resource Driver] measure of the consumption of a resource, used to determine the portion of the total resource cost assigned to each activity that uses the resource.

[Secondary activity] an activity that plays a supporting role to a primary activity.

[Strategic Management] a methodology for defining and achieving an enterprise's critical and long-term goals and objectives.

[Sustaining activity] an activity that supports the organization or the process as a whole.

[To-Be Model] a graphical representation of how a business process might be performed.

[Tracing] the assignment of resource costs to activities and activity costs to products based on an observable measure of the resources consumed or the activities performed.

[Value-Added Analysis] an analysis tool used to define the purpose and contribution of activities, evaluate the value they add, and guide the improvement efforts for each type of activity.

I N D E X

A   B   C   &   P

Accounting, Accounting Systems 6, 55, 117, 125, 126
Activity
    Primary 63-66
    Secondary 63-66
    Sustaining 63, 64, 106
Activity-Based Costing 1, 5-8, 117-120, 124-127
Activity-Based Performance 7, 15
Activity Cost Pool 11, 12, 58, 61, 106
Activity Model 37, 38, 41-47, 83, 88-93, 101-105, 114
Allocation 5, 18, 41, 47-50, 60-63, 106 108, 126
Alternatives 2, 4, 8, 33, 82, 87-90, 93, 97-105, 108, 109, 113, 123
Analysis 28, 31-34, 42-49, 56, 57, 73, 74, 77-99, 105, 108, 109
    Activity 105, 109
    Best Practices 85-88, 126
    Cost-Benefit 3, 97, 101, 117, 126
    Paradigm 77-79
    Pareto 74
    Performance-Based 3
    Value-Added 3, 79, 80
Baseline 4, 7, 12, 30, 37, 69, 108, 114
Benchmarking 3, 84-88, 126
Budgeting 6, 56, 127, 128
Business Improvement Analysis 4
Business Process Reengineering (BPR) 1-8, 11-15, 28-31, 34, 37, 38, 40, 64-68, 73-77, 83, 85, 88, 91-93, 97-101, 104, 108, 109, 113-120, 123, 124, 128
Computer-Aided Manufacturing Intl. (CAM-I) 8
Continuous Improvement 6, 8, 12, 57, 114, 116, 119, 120, 124
Controls 39, 45, 46, 102, 116, 118
Cost Element 58, 60
Cost Object 13-15
Cost Pool 58, 106
Cost Type 56
Culture 2, 116, 117, 120
Data 23-29, 37, 38, 42-44, 49, 51, 54, 85, 98-101, 106, 117, 125, 126
Data Sources 25
Documentation 25, 26, 58
Driver 81, 82, 88, 105, 106
    Activity 15, 16, 44, 47, 49-54, 64-69, 81, 106
    Cost 14, 16-18, 45, 50-54, 69, 81, 82, 108
    Resource 14, 45, 47-49, 54, 57-60, 69, 81

Functional Economic Analysis 4, 88, 99, 109
Functional Process Improvement 4
IDEFØ 39, 42-47, 88, 102, 105
Impacts, Process Change 101-104
Indirect Costs 48
Inputs 16, 17, 39, 47, 50, 51, 101-104, 118, 124
Interviews 25, 26, 41, 58, 61, 64
Mechanisms 39, 47, 102, 118
Metrics 85-87
Model 29, 33, 37-47, 56, 57, 83, 105, 116, 126
    Activity 27, 29-31, 37, 41, 101-105, 114
    As-Is 4, 33, 37-42, 56, 69, 73, 83, 89 91, 98, 105-109
    To-Be 4, 33, 73, 88-93, 98, 101, 103, 108, 109, 113, 116, 120
Non-Value Added 82-84
Outputs 38-47, 51-54, 79, 83, 101, 102, 104, 118, 124, 127
Paradigm - see Analysis - Paradigm
Performance, Performance Measures 1, 3, 5, 8, 12-18, 37, 44, 45, 51-56, 69, 73, 78, 81, 93, 98, 103, 104, 108, 109, 114-120, 124, 126, 128
Process Improvement 4, 114, 119, 120, 123
Product Cost 11, 12, 37, 44, 47, 48, 50, 56, 61, 66, 69, 126
Project Framework 4, 7, 23, 24, 34
Questionnaires 25, 27, 58, 66
Risk 98, 108, 116, 127
Simulation 90-93
Stakeholders 23-25
Strategic Planning, Strategic Management 5, 82, 123, 126
Teams 31-34
Tracing 47-50, 56, 59-64, 106, 108, 124
Value-Added 77-84, 88
Value-Added Analysis 3, 77-80
Workshops 25, 27, 33, 41, 58

A   M   S

Karen B. Burk

is a Senior Principal at American Management Systems, Inc. She manages the DoD process consulting practice area and was the primary developer of the Corporate Renewal Method,[sm] AMS's approach to business process reengineering.

Douglas W. Webster, Ph.D.,

is a Principal at American Management Systems, Inc. He did his doctoral research on Activity-Based Costing, and has previously published work on ABC and concurrent engineering, including several ABC case studies. He manages the AMS Activity-Based Costing and Performance consulting practice area, and is a frequent speaker on ABC, BPR, concurrent engineering, and performance measurement.

AMS is a leading international firm in helping clients strengthen performance. We work with our clients to achieve results, applying industry-specific expertise, technical insights, and proven methods and tools. Please call for further information on any of the following services and tools, or complete and mail the attached postcard.

Consulting Services:

- Activity-Based Costing
- Performance Measurement
- Quality Management
- Business Process Reengineering

Training Services:

- Executive Seminar on ABC&P
- Implementing ABC&P
- Government Performance and Results Act Overview
- Government Performance and Results Act Implementation Planning
- Business Process Reengineering

Tools:

- Performance Measurement Desktop Software

To order additional copies of this book, call **1-800-879-4214.**

To request further information on consulting and training services, please write or call:

American Management Systems, Inc.
ABC&P Group
4050 Legato Road
Fairfax, VA 22033
Telephone: (703) 267-5500, Fax: (703) 841-5507.

AMS is a leading firm in helping clients strengthen performance. AMS has completed over two decades of consecutive growth and has offices in 29 cities in North America and seven cities in Europe.

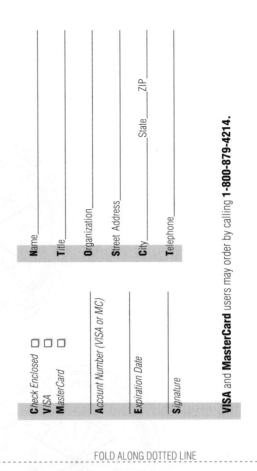

Name

Title

Organization

Street Address

City _____ State ____ ZIP

Telephone

Check Enclosed ☐
VISA ☐
MasterCard ☐

Account Number (VISA or MC)

Expiration Date

Signature

VISA and **MasterCard** users may order by calling **1-800-879-4214.**

FOLD ALONG DOTTED LINE

Please send me more information on the following (check all that apply):

Training Services

_____ Executive Seminar on ABC&P
_____ Implementing ABC&P
_____ Government Performance and Results Act Overview
_____ Government Performance and Results Act Implementation Planning
_____ Business Process Reengineering

Tools

_____ Performance Measurement Desktop Software

Please send me _____ copies (hardcover) of the ABC&P handbook at $39.95 per copy plus $3.95 for postage and handling each, totaling $ _____. Please allow four to six weeks for delivery. For bulk orders of 20 or more books, call 703-267-5500.

BOOKCRAFTERS DISTRIBUTION CENTER

615 EAST INDUSTRIAL DRIVE

CHELSEA, MI 48118

FOLD ALONG DOTTED LINE

American Management Systems